RAGS to
RETIREMENT

RAGS to RETIREMENT

*Stories From People Who Retired Well
On Much Less Than You'd Think*

Gail Liberman and Alan Lavine

iUniverse, Inc.
Bloomington

Rags To Retirement
Stories From People Who Retired Well On
Much Less Than You'd Think

Copyright © 2010 by Gail Liberman and Alan Lavine

All rights reserved. No part of this book may be used or reproduced by any means, graphic, electronic, or mechanical, including photocopying, recording, taping or by any information storage retrieval system without the written permission of the publisher except in the case of brief quotations embodied in critical articles and reviews.

The information, ideas, and suggestions in this book are not intended to render professional advice. Before following any suggestions contained in this book, you should consult your personal accountant or other financial advisor. Neither the author nor the publisher shall be liable or responsible for any loss or damage allegedly arising as a consequence of your use or application of any information or suggestions in this book.

iUniverse books may be ordered through booksellers or by contacting:

iUniverse
1663 Liberty Drive
Bloomington, IN 47403
www.iuniverse.com
1-800-Authors (1-800-288-4677)

Because of the dynamic nature of the Internet, any Web addresses or links contained in this book may have changed since publication and may no longer be valid. The views expressed in this work are solely those of the author and do not necessarily reflect the views of the publisher, and the publisher hereby disclaims any responsibility for them.

Any people depicted in stock imagery provided by Thinkstock are models, and such images are being used for illustrative purposes only.

Certain stock imagery © Thinkstock.

ISBN: 978-1-4502-7687-0 (sc)
ISBN: 978-1-4502-7688-7 (ebk)

Printed in the United States of America

iUniverse rev. date: 12/4/2010

This book is dedicated to our uncle, Herman "Gene" Liberman, whose creative retirement helped inspire us to write this book.

Contents

1. Elizabeth and William J. Schrader: Living It Up South of the Border!. 1
2. Thomas "Tom" Murphy: Sailing Away in Retirement. 19
3. Herman "Gene" Liberman: Dancing Around the World 33
4. Duane and Dolores "Dee" Mark: Building Their Dream Retirement Home 47
5. Edgar and Betty Plunkett: Retiring Early in Belize. 61
6. Alan and Sandra Clark: King and Queen of the Road 75
7. Victor and Ruth Barnard: Livening Up the Neighborhood . . .91
8. Alejandro "Alex" and Letty Monforte: Immigrants Parlay Job Benefits into the Good Life 107
9. Larry and Kris Ferstenou: Planning Early Did the Trick. 123
10. Dennis Hastings: Native American Antrhopologist Beating Stroke 133
11. Kathleen Maddox: Reversal of Fortune 147
12. Vicki and Paul Terhorst: A new Breed of Retiree—Perpetual Travelers 157

Epilogue 171

About the Authors. 175

Introduction

It would be nice to retire knowing that we have a small fortune backing us up! Unfortunately, the overwhelming majority of us don't have this luxury. As our book went to press, this cold, stark fact seemed to hit especially hard. The United States was trying to bail out of a three-year bear market in stocks. At the same time, the nation's baby boomers have been reaching their 50s and 60s—the very ages at which their parents retired before them. Yet, for way too many in this feisty, trend-setting generation, the promise of what was expected to be a nouveau wave of retirement has fizzled to little more than a pipe dream. Savings and social security just don't seem like enough.

Our goal is to prove that, with a little know-how and creativity, this needn't be the case. No matter what your age, it is possible to successfully retire with a net worth of much less than $1 million—regardless of what the financial magazines and financial planners say. Okay, we admit that we wrote two other books based on a totally different concept. *Rags to Riches* and *More Rags to Riches,* both published by Dearborn, showed how ordinary people went from being poor to having a net worth of at least $1 million. In those books, we heavily probed our subjects to find out exactly how they did it. With this book, however, we decided to devote the same amount of energy to proving that you don't necessarily need $1 million to retire comfortably. We probed even harder to find out what else you can do to retire—without necessarily raking in the big bucks.

Even if you are in your 50s and 60s, it's never too late to save. Every little bit helps. Many of the people in our book had a little savings, maybe an annuity or a small pension. The income from their savings and social security did go far.

We have combed the world in search of people who may not necessarily have much money. But the one thing they had in common is that they all had the guts to retire and live fulfilling, creative and inspiring lives. We wanted to hear in their own words exactly how they did it, how they feel, and how they're managing.

We wanted to share their tips and the lessons they learned. With this book, we also go one step further than we did with our other *Rags* books. We explain, with the help of renowned experts, exactly what you can do to implement similar strategies. We wanted to show you the ropes of what is involved. Plus, we wanted to make sure you avoid any major mistakes. Our book also offers practical tips in each chapter on how you, too, can retire creatively on the money you have amassed over the years. We tell where you might find resources you need to achieve this goal.

For example, Duane and Dee Mark have very little to live on. But while Duane was working, he bought a parcel of land in Arizona. Duane was building his own home with solar heat. He and his wife fully expected to live comfortably in their senior years. When we reached them, they had fallen upon hard times, but they were on their way to accomplishing their goal.

Others, like Edgar and Betty Plunkett, are financially well off compared to many people. The couple bought a waterfront home in Belize, a Central American country, and retired in 1999 with about a half-million dollars. A half-million dollars may sound like a lot. But at today's interest rates, the income from the investments would not have gone very far had the couple remained in their beachfront condo in Carolina Beach, North Carolina. The couple reports that they found it more than $300 a week cheaper to live in Belize than in North Carolina.

Tom Murphy took a different route. The retired post office worker lives on a sailboat. His home base is Boston Harbor. But he travels up and down the East Coast. Tom combined sailing, the joy of his life, with a lower cost of living. Renting an apartment in Boston can cost more than $1,500 per month. Meanwhile, condos cost well over $300,000. Tom saves a fortune living on his boat. More important, he is happy and lives life to its fullest. He has friends in every marina, from Maine to Florida. In addition, he has a terrific backyard.

What This Book Is ... and Isn't

This book is nothing like any of the "how to" retirement books currently on the shelves. Those generally offer formulas on how to budget and invest to arrive at a prescribed amount for retirement. More people

Introduction

should read those books and follow the advice. Yet, most people never truly reach those goals—as many, unfortunately, are learning a bit late in their lives. Statistics don't lie. According to *The Wall Street Journal*, roughly half of workers on private payrolls don't even have an employer-sponsored retirement plan!

Instead of a how-to retire book, we merely seek to provide you with 12 entertaining chapters, each spotlighting a named retiree or retired couple who have managed to live creatively with limited resources. The people in our book come from all age groups, geographic regions, and ethnic backgrounds. They include people who retired early, those who collect Social Security, and those who are not yet eligible for Social Security. We continue to believe that there is no better way to learn about the finances of retiring than to learn from others who already have managed them.

Rags to Retirement focuses on an extremely wide range of people. Some have retired with virtually nothing in their bank accounts. Some have $750,000. Others may be living on $1,000 to $2,000 per month, including Social Security. None of this is very much when you consider the cost of living and the rapid increase in inflation, not to mention how long we are all living now! The bulk of retiree expenses today goes to rapidly rising medical insurance, drug costs, and other health-care costs. Nevertheless those in our book have found a way to stretch their dollars and live meaningful lives.

This book serves up real-life experience with which you can compare your situation. You will learn from people in their own words how they achieved a successful retirement and how they live within their means. Maybe you will get some ideas from the experiences of the people we interviewed. If you find yourself identifying with their situations, you can learn from their mistakes as well as their accomplishments.

We've been through a tough economic recession that has stock market investments and retirement savings plans down as much as 40 percent. The bottom line today: The overwhelming majority of the nation's population is fearful that it lacks adequate funds for a comfortable retirement. Unfortunately, reports indicate that most people don't have the savings to realize their retirement dreams.

The median household's net worth is a mere $86,000, according to the Federal Reserve. The U.S. savings rate is just beginning to climb. In addition, the average account size of a 401 (k) company pension plan is just $40,000.

Often when a person reaches a certain age, financial advisers can do little to turn the situation around. Say you stop working and want to live on a mere $50,000 a year, excluding social security. You'd need $833,000 in retirement savings— assuming that the account paid 6 percent annually. Realistically, that may be beyond the realm of most of us unless we already have made some extreme financial sacrifices.

Can we make back those losses in the 2000, 2001, and 2002 stock markets? Hopefully, but it could take years. No one knows for sure how the stock market will perform. In 1972 and 1973, when the stock market lost about 45 percent, it took more than five years to break even on those losses. Bank CDs and money market accounts are yielding less than 2 percent. Incomes are down compared with five years ago, but the costs of rent, food, utilities, transportation, health care, and property taxes are rising. Hopefully, interest rates will rise a little so that retirees can earn more income.

The younger you are, the more you can invest in stocks for growth. You need the extra time to make back any losses. Financial planners say that even retirees should have at least 20 percent of their assets in stocks. The reason: Stocks have historically returned about 7 percent more than inflation. So it still could pay to keep some money in blue-chip, high dividend-yielding common stock mutual funds. The investment should help maintain your purchasing power over the years.

One problem: You have to invest in the stock market through thick and thin. Unfortunately, according to a study by Dalbar, Inc., in Boston, most people don't do that.

Meanwhile, for those who are significantly older, stocks present a very risky option. To realize the long-term benefits of higher returns, experts say you need to invest a minimum of 10 years.

For baby boomers in or near their 60s, it is nearly impossible to safely save anywhere near $1 million in the little time they have left! Many are strapped with debt, expenses, children, and aging parents to support. Even a $500,000 retirement nest egg is outside the reach of most middle-class Americans.

Ruefully, financial advisers have told us that many who would like to retire changed their plans during the recent economic recession. They believe that they simply don't have enough money saved. We personally have run into a number of retired people who have gone back to work part-time so that they could make ends meet.

We wrote *Rags to Retirement* to present you with a totally different perspective on retirement. A fulfilling retirement doesn't always require a seven-digit net worth. There are creative ways out there to hang up your spikes and still live a happy and healthy life.

Rags to Retirement communicates in retirees' own words strategies that successfully have overcome financial limitations.

We hope you enjoy and learn something from the people in this book. We certainly did.

Books by Gail Liberman and Alan Lavine

Rags to Riches: Motivating Stories of How Ordinary People Achieved Extraordinary Wealth!
More Rags to Riches: All New Stories of How Ordinary People Achieved Extraordinary Wealth
The Complete Idiot's Guide to Making Money with Mutual Funds
Improving Your Credit and Reducing Your Debt
Love, Marriage, and Money
Short and Simple Guide to Life Insurance
Short and Simple Guide to Smart Investing

Books by Alan Lavine

Your Life Insurance Options
Diversify Your Way to Wealth
Getting Started in Mutual Funds
Diversify: Investors' Guide to Asset Allocation Strategies

Acknowledgments

We'd like to thank our editor, Mike Sanders, of Alpha Books, for making this book possible.

We also thank all the people in our book, who chatted with us for hours strictly so that you—the reader—would fully understand exactly how to retire—regardless of how little money you have. Our sincerest gratitude goes to Elizabeth and William J. Schrader, Tom Murphy, Herman "Gene" Liberman, Duane and Dolores "Dee" Mark, Edgar and Betty Plunkett, Alan and Sandra Clark, Victor and Ruth Barnard, Alejandro "Alex" and Letty Monforte, Larry A. and Kris Ferstenou, and Dennis Hastings and Kathleen Maddox.

We also can't forget the many experts we contacted—often on extremely short notice. Our thanks go to: Stephen Yale-Loehr, who teaches immigration law at Cornell University, Ithaca, New York; Andrew Kochera, senior policy advisor for AARP, Washington D.C.; Laird Schaub, executive secretary for the Fellowship for Intentional Community, Rutledge, Missouri; Marjorie Marlin, executive director of Cooperative Housing Corp., Somerville, New Jersey; Rita Zadoff, co-president of the National Shared Housing Resource Center, Atlanta; Gaylord Maxwell, founder and president of the Life on Wheels school, Moscow, Idaho; Wynema Morris, a tribal member and permanent staff researcher for the Omaha Tribal Historical Research Project; Chris Stainbrook, president of the nonprofit Indian Land Tenure Foundation, Little Canada, Missouri; Stanley F. Denman, a Dallas-based social security disability attorney; Ken Scholen, reverse mortgage specialist with the AARP, Washington, D.C.; Glenn Petherick, director of communications for the National Reverse Mortgage Lenders Association, Washington, D.C.; New York elder law attorney Peter J. Strauss; J. Stephen Wilson, co-author of "Win the Green Card Lottery" (Self-Counsel Press); Richard M. Stephens, land use regulations attorney in Bellevue, Washington; Andrew J. Goldstein, Newark, New Jersey attorney specializing in maritime law; Don D. Nelson, tax attorney and certified public accountant in Dana Point, California; Jeffrey D. Hill, certified financial planner with LPL Financial Services, Inc., Denver; Mark Landon, owner ofShipsjobs.com and publisher of "Cruise Ship Crews," Fort Lauderdale, Florida; Lemar Wooley, spokesman for the U.S. Department of Housing and Urban Development, Washington, D.C.; Ron Pollack, executive director of Families USA, Washington, D.C.; David Connell, a corporate foreign investment lawyer in Ixtapa, Guerrero, Mexico; and Tor Pinney, author *oi Ready for Sea! How to Outfit the Modern Cruising Sailboat* (Sheridan House).

Chapter 1

Elizabeth and William J. Schrader: Living It Up South of the Border!

Elizabeth "Betty" and William J. "Bill" Schrader live the retired "Life of Riley" in beautiful Lake Chapala, Mexico. All right, there are a few inconveniences. But their income of just over $2,000 monthly from Social Security and fixed annuities goes a long way compared with back in the States.

It was a bold move for the couple in 1993. They sold the home they had lived in for 25 years in Elk River, Minnesota, for $85,000; auctioned their furniture; and moved to Mexico. Their net worth: less than $225,000.

The couple had been married 39 years when we talked to them and previously worked in Minneapolis for Honeywell International. Bill, 74, was an engineer, and Betty, 72, worked in cost accounting and procurement. Upon retirement, Bill had a choice of taking his pension in a lump sum or having it annuitized monthly. His financial adviser told him it would . stand a better chance of keeping up with inflation if he took the lump sum and invested it.

So, they are living off Social Security and a little income from annuities. When we talked with them from their newer home in San Nicolas de Ibarra, Jalisco, the couple said that their income "slightly" covers their expenses.

For the first time, this retired couple has the luxury of a private swimming pool, a weekly maid, and a gardener. The cost is cheap: $5 weekly for four hours of maid service and $25 a week for the gardener, who comes three days a week.

They have been able to say good-bye to the whopping heating and air-conditioning bills they experienced in their previous home near Minneapolis. No more snow blowers, winterizing of cars, or expensive storm windows, either. Extra clothes—boots, gloves, mittens, and winter coats—have become largely a thing of the past. They estimate that their monthly expenses would be at least $1,000 per month higher had they remained in the United States.

Today Betty sets her alarm clock for three days a week instead of five to do volunteer work for the Lake Chapala Society, believed to be the world's largest group of expatriates. Typically, she goes to lunch with a friend or her husband one day weekly. She also enjoys sewing, doing computer work, reading, and watching television.

Bill sits on three different boards of directors for free— including the board of the 3,000-member Lake Chapala Society, his residents association, and the Hack Foundation, which donates money to humane societies. You might say that the man who has two engineering degrees has done an about-face from what used to be a very structured life. He recently received a royalty check from his first romance novel, *Kiss My Tears Away* (Booksurge). When we contacted him, he was working on another.

"Since we moved down here, my husband has blossomed," Betty observes. "He tended to be a very quiet person in the States. If we were at a party, I would not say he was a wallflower, but he tended not to be at the center of every conversation. Since we moved here, he has been more talkative, outgoing, and friendly. He's changed—and all for the better. I don't know if retirement would have done that for him in the States. I think it's been good for both of us."

Bill admits that when he first came to Mexico, he was apprehensive. It was a new language and a new culture, but a far cry from the high-pressure life he had been working to support a wife and family. "As a person, I was thrust into a new universe," he says. "I didn't have to prove anything. I could just be myself. I didn't have to rely on anybody to give me an income. That whole scenario helps to create a new self-confidence."

The couple actually considered retiring in the States and took the advice of an acquaintance who suggested planning their retirement five years in advance. They purchased a book on the best places to retire in the States. However, they subsequently came upon a small article in a Sunday newspaper discussing how U.S. citizens were moving to foreign countries and living attractive lifestyles.

They already had vacationed in Monterrey, Mexico, in 1967 and had stayed in Puerto Vallarta some seven years before their final move. The Puerto Vallarta trip had been linked to Bill's career. "We liked the whole Mexican mystique," Betty says. Among the other areas they had considered for their retirement were Costa Del Sol, Spain, and Costa Rica.

Following the article's suggestion, they sent to Guadalajara for a newsletter. They mulled it over for six months before they decided to go down and look around. They chose Mexico at least partially because of its proximity to the United States. "I have an elderly sister who lives alone in New Mexico," Betty explains. "Also, if we did not like living here, the move to the States would be considerably easier than if we had lived elsewhere."

The Schraders actually retired three years earlier than they thought they would and made another trip to Guadalajara. They discussed their possible move with their two daughters, who encouraged them. Bill retired in January 1993, and Betty retired five months later. They sold their home and, by June, packed up their rental truck and drove to Mexico via Betty's sister house in Albuquerque. They soon found themselves living in another country.

The Schraders had no intention of immediately buying another house. Instead, they obtained a visa for six months and initially rented. They rented the home that they currently own for four years before finally purchasing it for $165,000 around 1998 with some of the proceeds of Betty's annuity. The previous owners, who disliked living in Mexico, had moved back to the States and offered to credit four years of rent toward the purchase price. It was an offer that the Schraders could not refuse. They used a real estate agent they knew to help with the transaction. Their two-bedroom masonry brick and stone home, which sits on about a half acre in a gated community of some 130 homes, has a library/computer room, a full kitchen, and four full baths. There also is a *casita,* or self-contained guest house that sleeps four. Today, they estimate their home would be worth close to a quarter-million dollars in the United States.

"Having lived most of our lives in the northern Midwest, I still am amazed at flowering trees," Betty says. "I love flowers!" Their home has floor-to-ceiling windows overlooking Lake Chapala, mountains, and, in the distance, the Colima volcano. "I'm looking out on bougainvillea-covered walls, a golf range, and green trees," she says. "Our neighbors have banana and avocado trees." Films of Mexico often show sand and cactus, but both spouses say they have no idea where those come from.

Betty and Bill Schrader both drive in Mexico. Betty drives a 1989 Toyota Corolla, and Bill drives a 1992 Toyota Previa van. The two say they speak Spanish *"mas* or *menos,"* and Bill voluntarily teaches conversational English to Mexicans.

The Schraders immigrated to Mexico in the FM3 immigration category. That's a category that Bill often advises when people inquire about moving to Mexico. The FM2 might carry a higher status largely because it requires a higher income, but Bill says the FM3 has fewer restrictions.

With an FM2, you achieve immigration status and don't have to renew, but you are required to drive a Mexican-plated car, which means you have to sell your car and buy a car in Mexico, he says. "That doubles your car insurance (cost), and you have to pay taxes on the car. We advise everybody to go for the FM3 because they can drive American cars." The FM3 category, however, must be periodically renewed.

When the couple prepared to move, they inquired of the Mexican consulate what papers they would need. They were given a list of items that included birth certificates, a marriage license, and a letter from a doctor. "When we got down here and put in for the FM3, the only thing they were interested in was the marriage license," Bill says. This was the couple's first experience dealing with some of the oddities of Mexican regulations. Another example came more recently. The Mexican government decided that, by the end of January 2003, everybody would need to register to obtain a special number, similar to a Social Security number in the United States. The number was designed to make it easier to administer public services. But when it was announced that those with a bank account would need to register for this number, confusion reigned.

One thing about Mexico, Betty says, is that if enough people express concern about something, the government listens. At this writing, during the deadline month, the most recent newspaper account indicated that people needn't worry about the controversial number—at least for the time being. The January deadline likely would be extended, if the requirement even remained intact.

In Guadalajara, Betty reflects, the government also backed down on at least two occasions when proposed actions ruffled the feathers of area farmers. "All the farmers got together and drove tractors, farm vehicles, and animals right up to the capital building in Guadalajara," she says. "They clogged traffic, and the government decided that maybe it didn't want to do that."

On the other side of the coin, she says, a police officer didn't back down from citing her for an alleged violation after she went through a yellow light. She was not guilty, she says. But to avoid a problem, she offered the officer 200 pesos, or $20. "It was near Easter," Betty explains. "Easter is bigger down here than Christmas, and police probably needed money for whatever. I was not really guilty, but when they pull you over, there you are." The couple says that another police officer friend of theirs later advised that they could have gotten away with paying the officer just 20 pesos, or $2. "I suspect it's different in every town," she says.

However, if you come to Mexico thinking that you can bribe your way out of a traffic violation or any type of law enforcement problem, don't be so sure, Betty warns. A recent article in the newspaper indicated that a crackdown on bribery was underway. A local official had warned that anyone offering a bribe to a police officer would be as guilty as the officer who accepted it. "They were very, very low paid," Betty says of the police. "(The government) is trying to stamp this out."

***

You might think that at the Schraders' age, they would be concerned about obtaining medical care in a foreign country. The Schraders pay about $200 monthly for Blue Cross/Blue Shield, one of the very few U.S. health insurance providers that covers Americans living outside the country. Medicare does not provide insurance in foreign countries. Nevertheless, the Schraders continue to have the cost of Medicare deducted from their Social Security payments each month—-just in case they ever prefer to be treated in the United States.

Both spouses say they already have had serious surgeries in Mexico and could not have been treated better—at about one quarter of the cost that their surgeries might have cost in the States. "They solved the problem 110 percent," Bill declared of the laminectomy he had due to calcium build-up inside the vertebrae of his neck. "I had an appointment at the Mayo Clinic. At the last minute, I changed my mind and had it done down here." The surgery was effective, he says. But that wasn't all. When he was admitted to the hospital for surgery on a Sunday night—the day before—two neurosurgeons and an anesthesiologist came in to greet him and check on his well-being.

"They treat you more like a human being than an insurance number," Betty says. "They are seriously concerned about your mental welfare." Many American retirees lack faith in the Mexican doctors and travel to the United States for major surgery, Bill acknowledges. "This country, like the United States, has good doctors and bad doctors." He admits, though, that he had his surgery at San Javier Hospital in Guadalajara—about a half-hour drive from where they live—because he was able to obtain specialists there. He likens that situation to when he was living in Elk River, Minnesota. There, he often drove to Minneapolis for his specialized medical care.

They admit that some things require getting used to in Mexico. They have no dishwasher—a convenience that Betty misses particularly when she has a lot of company. Also, there's no garbage disposal. At an altitude of 5,200 feet, they have no heat or air-conditioning. Although the weather often is in the 70s, sometimes they need to use electric blankets or electric heaters. Plus, the country has scorpions, which can pack a deadly sting. In fact, Betty saw one on a day we interviewed her, and Bill has been stung twice. "I was picking a towel up at the pool that had been laying out all night," he says of the first incident. The scorpion was hiding under the towel. Provided that you have no allergies to a scorpion sting, it simply requires taking an antihistamine, he says. The Schraders also spray for scorpions around their house. "The first time I got stung on the hand, it started to go up my arm," Bill said. "I drove to the Red Cross and they gave me a shot. No big deal."

The Schraders' Social Security and other income is deposited electronically into Wells Fargo Bank, which has a branch in Albuquerque, New Mexico, near the home of Betty's sister. Through Bill's checking account, he writes checks that he cashes at Lloyd Group, a Mexico investment house. "We do not put a lot of money in the banks down here," he stresses. Interest rates are unusually high, but there can be problems if you need to convert pesos into dollars. In 1994, the peso was devalued. While interest on one account zoomed, a friend who was attempting to change his Mexican currency to U.S. dollars lost $60,000. The losses stemmed only from converting the pesos back to dollars. If you never intend to convert pesos to dollars, they say, there likely will be no problem keeping your money in a Mexico institution.

The couple has a financial adviser from Minneapolis who has since moved to Palm Springs, California. Lloyd Group pays their electric and phone bills. "That saves me from standing in line," Bill says.

Be careful when buying property in Mexico, the Schraders advise. "You don't have the title protection down here that you have in the States," Bill warns. "Somebody could sell you a bag of goods, and you're stuck." The couple found an excellent real estate agent, whom they are convinced knows all the pros and cons of buying property. It is critical in any foreign country that you find reliable professionals. "Ask the same questions of at least six people," Betty advises. "That way, you can find a competent doctor, dentist, real estate agent, or lawyer. It's very important in any foreign country to know who are the good guys and who are the bad guys."

Perhaps one of the greatest downsides to living in Mexico has been the rapidly increasing cost of living. "Too many gringos (foreigners)," Bill says.

The problem, according to Betty, is that people move down from places like California, where they might be paying $50 for a gardener. When they find that they can get a gardener for two weeks for the same amount that it costs for one week back home, often they remark how cheap it is. "Mexican people are not stupid," she says. "If somebody says, 'Is that all?,' they're going to raise their price. Prices have risen in this area. They will continue to raise prices as long as the gringos will pay."

The couple stresses that although they have a Blue Cross/ Blue Shield plan, many insurance companies in the States will not cover American policyholders in Mexico. "It's sad because the insurance companies would pay less if they covered people there," Betty says.

She remembers going to a doctor for a sore throat. The bill came to $25. On the other hand, she remembers paying $86 in the States when she had a sore throat and had the doctor check her ear.

"One year ago, I had a wisdom tooth pulled," Bill says. "The (Mexican) dentist said he would have somebody else do it. Who does it, but a neurosurgeon? The whole thing cost me about $40. I never felt a thing from start to finish."

Betty also mentions that some of her prescriptions are cheaper than in the United States. Only certain drugs require prescriptions in Mexico.

At this writing, the two say that it is considerably less expensive to eat out in Mexico than in the United States. She recalls that her husband's surprise birthday party for 15 had cost just $120 in Mexico two years ago—$39 cheaper than a more recent restaurant dinner for five in Minnesota. "All had drinks and ordered what they wanted to eat, which was not inexpensive Mexican food," she said of the Mexican experience. In Minnesota, just one person had beer and two had mixed drinks. "No filet mignon or anything terribly expensive was served and two desserts were shared by four." The Mexico restaurant price, she stressed, would be about the same today. Also, produce grown in Mexico is very cheap. Yet, the couple has access to the "Big Four": Costco, Wal-mart, Sam's Club, and a fourth superstore in one shopping center in Guadalajara. The couple has learned to shop in local Mexican grocery stores or to buy in bulk. Paying in pesos rather than dollars often can garner a better price. They generally take one trip annually, usually by car, to the United States.

One frustration that Bill has experienced living in Mexico is that it's difficult to get snafus corrected. Once, when the couple was away in Italy visiting one of their daughters, the electric company changed the electric meter at their home. Five times they had tried to turn it off for nonpayment of a bill. Lloyd Group, which had been paying the couple's electric bill, had not been notified. "It was a big hassle to get everything straightened out," Bill says. It turned out that the company had incorrectly billed them both for the meter they had replaced and for the new meter. The company finally returned half the money. But generally with public companies, there is no one to complain to if you have a problem.

Betty says that one organization, Link, maintains a desk at the Lake Chapala Society. It has a representative who speaks fluent Spanish and will intervene to straighten out such snafus.

At the other end of the spectrum, the couple has found excellent mechanics, many of whom will write off charges for certain services or charge extraordinarily low fees. If you are dissatisfied, they don't think twice about rectifying something without a charge.

It's true that most Mexicans in this region speak English. Yet, "you have to be prepared to go with the flow," Betty says. "You cannot come down to this country or any country with a mind-set that you're going to do and have what you had in the States. Laws are different. Culture is different. In certain respects, the food is different. The Mexican people are much more family-oriented than any place we've ever been." It is not uncommon for a business to close for the day because an aunt is sick or a child is sick. While gringos just walked by the Schraders once when they had a flat tire, a Mexican ran to help them change it.

Betty advises that anyone coming to the area should rent first. The environment, which has become a major cause in the United States, is not yet a priority in Mexico, although it is being worked on. Some people are outraged by the waste paper sitting around and the lack of garbage treatment, she says. "There are things down here that can be annoying if it's an issue with a person. Come down and rent for a minimum of six months. It can be a culture shock."

The couple has a computer and uses e-mail. Betty's sister in Albuquerque gets some mail and sends it down. "It's slow," Betty says. "The phone service isn't as good as in the States. We have a rainy season in mid-June through the first of November. Very often, for whatever reason we don't totally understand, the phones will be out." So when you live in Mexico, she says, you must keep an oil lamp and candles in the house.

Property taxes are extraordinarily low. Last year's property taxes for the Schraders' home totaled $50. They pay no income tax. But they pay a 15 percent sales tax, although it's not levied on groceries or medicines. Their homeowners fees, paid quarterly, tallied $280 in a recent quarter. It varies, though, based on usage of services, which include the security guard, water, street lighting, and maintenance of the common elements.

If you're considering moving to Mexico, Betty advises that you read as much a possible. "Do not accept any book that says you can live down here on blank amount of money a month!" she warns. "Nine out of 10 are outdated. No one's lifestyle is like any one else's. You should try to e-mail people who live here and have lived here for a while and will give honest information. That's part of my job."

She also warns that although there are websites describing life in certain areas, many do not tell the whole truth. For example, thanks to some published reports, many think that the Lake Chapala Society offers a group medical insurance policy. Not so. Instead, very economical medical insurance is available through the Instituto Mexicano del Seguro Social (IMMS). However, warns Betty, "you can only go to certain doctors. If you want to see a specialist, you might have a long wait."

It's too bad, she says. Many of those moving to Mexico are over 50—which is the age that medical insurance starts to get expensive. "If insurance companies in the States would cover medical bills, the whole country would save a lot of money." It definitely would be cheaper for insurance companies than having their policyholders get treated at more expensive U.S. doctors and hospitals.

Doing It Yourself

What if you want to retire somewhere other than in the United States? It can be done. The Schraders estimate that they are saving $1,000 monthly living south of the border. And most important, their lifestyle has improved. You need to do a great deal before you consider moving anywhere abroad. You've got to research the best areas to live. It's also not a bad idea to vacation in an area first to check everything out. And be sure to talk to Americans who currently live in a country you are considering. Get the pros and the cons of life as a retired expatiate.

Get a fix on your income and expenses. Check the value of an area's currency, which generally is published weekly in most major newspapers. But keep in mind that currency values can fluctuate dramatically. What looks cheap now may not be as cheap tomorrow. We know people who live part of the year in France. While prices in France previously were cheaper than in the United States, thanks to the fluctuating currency values, things rapidly have gotten more expensive.

If you are receiving any retirement benefits, contact the agency that is issuing them to determine how you can continue to receive your benefits in another country. Make arrangements for direct deposit of any investment or social security income; checks can be stolen.

You can find a wealth of information, including consular reports and a list of country consulates, on the website of the U.S. State Department at www.state.gov. Check the same website for terrorism alerts, or call the Office of Overseas Citizens Services, at 202-647-5225. Make sure you understand the visa policies of the country and requirements for residency by calling the country's consulate.

Evaluate a country's health-care system. Make arrangements for medical insurance in your new abode. Then get dental, eye, and medical check-ups before you leave; don't forget to ask your doctor about the appropriate vaccinations and shots. Check the website of the U.S. Centers for Disease Control, at www.cdc.gov, for medical alerts.

The following are additional tips on settling abroad:
- If possible, learn the language before you move.
- Understand the tax situation of the country.
- Evaluate the climate and activities of the area.
- Research how widespread crime is.

We found a great website, www.expatexchange.com, with message boards that let you chat with expatriates who live in the area of your choice. Other websites worth visiting are www.internationalliving.com, www.escapeartist.com, and www. expatforum. com.

Health-Care Issues Abroad

Health care may be the greatest issue for retirees both here and abroad. If you are over 65, you cannot use Medicare benefits overseas. So, if you are considering overseas retirement, you might want to hold on to your old company's health-care coverage. Check your overseas benefits with your former employer's human resources group, advises David Feng, spokesman for CIGNA HealthCare in Bloomfield, Connecticut. At CIGNA HealthCare, for example, "usually all emergency care and urgent care is covered," he says. However, the company does not issue individual policies to American retirees living overseas. You might be able to obtain medical insurance at a low cost under an arrangement with the country to which you are moving.

Some countries offer national health care or a combination of national or private health insurance. Retirees in Mexico can get low-cost coverage from the Institute Mexicano del Seguro Social (IMSS). Unfortunately, not many U.S. health insurance companies provide coverage for American retirees living abroad. Some Blue Cross/Blue Shield plans are reported to be among the few. Many retirees who live in Latin, Central, and South America instead fly to the United States for medical problems.

The good news is that you can get international major medical health insurance much more cheaply if you're living in another country than you could if you lived in the United States. A husband age 55 and wife age 52 might pay $1,698 annually for international health insurance coverage with a $1,000 deductible, or $141.50 a month for both. By contrast, the same couple living in the United States would pay $4,800 to $6,000 a year, or $400 to $500 monthly, for coverage.

You'll want to probe the broker or person who sells you international insurance for safety ratings of a company you are selecting, and examine the policy for exclusions, insurance limits, and deductibles. You'll want to know whether it covers both routine and emergency treatment, hospitalization, and medical evacuation in case you need urgent medical care in a remote area. The U.S. State Department warns that medical evacuation can cost more than $10,000.

Finding Good International Health-Care Coverage

Are you squeamish about giving up your U.S. health insurance coverage? If you check the World Health Organization at www.who.int, your mind might change. The organization rates 176 countries on the quality and efficiency of their health-care services. Based on the rankings at this writing, the United States was pretty far down on the ladder, ranking thirty-seventh. The World Health Organization ranked France and Italy first and second, respectively, as having the best health-care coverage. Hot retirement spots include Spain, ranked seventh; Portugal, ranked twelfth; Ireland, ranked nineteenth; Cyprus, ranked twenty-fourth; Costa Rica, ranked thirty-sixth; Mexico, ranked fifty-first; and Belize, ranked sixty-ninth.

You can get coverage, excluding the United States, from a number of international health insurance companies. For example, Medibroker (www.medibroker.com) is a U.K. insurance broker that will help you find international insurance coverage. Many of the international healthcare policies are underwritten by Lloyds of London. You can live in any region of the world and get comprehensive or partial coverage.

These companies provide international health insurance:
- a A La Carte Health Care www.alchealth.corn
  Allianz Worldwide Care
- www.allianzworldwidecare.com
  BUPA International www.bupa-intl.com
- Expacare
  www.expacare.net
- Healthcare International
  www.healthcareinternational.com
- InterGlobal International Private Healthcare
  www.medical-insurance-interglobal.co.uk
- International Medical Group www.imglobal.com
- William Russell Group International Health Plan
  www. william-r ussell .com

Don't Forget to Pay Your Taxes

Medibroker provides tax- and financial-planning services to expatriate retirees. You also can check with the Financial Planning Association (www.fpa.com) for a list of certified financial planners (CFP) who provide overseas services to U.S. citizens. Or, check with your local accountant and attorney before you leave the country for the names of experienced people who can help you with your financial affairs while you live abroad.

The good news is that if you retire to Mexico, you still can collect social security from the United States. The bad news is that you can't completely abandon Uncle Sam when it comes to your U.S. income taxes. "The biggest problem is, people all leave the United States and they assume they don't have to file tax returns because they're no longer there," says Don D. Nelson, a tax attorney and certified public accountant in Dana Point, California. "Then they decide to come back and live here, or they're going to inherit money. They suddenly find out the rules."

Nelson advises that you check the requirements for filing income taxes in both the United States and your new country of residence. Don't listen to what your Canadian friends say, either, he warns. Rules of the United States are very different from those of other countries. Just because you must file income taxes in the United States and the country to which you've moved doesn't necessarily mean that you'll pay double taxes. The United States has tax treaties with more than 60 countries, designed to avoid double taxation. Also, you may qualify for tax credits that can be used toward your U.S. taxes. But you still must file!

In the United States, the statute of limitations never runs out if you fail to file your income tax return. So, there's no limit on when you could be caught. Meanwhile, if you marry or renew your passport, it's possible that your Social Security number could be shared with the IRS. "You could be gone from the United States for 20 years," Nelson says. "If you didn't file a return for any particular year, the IRS could suddenly show up and say, 'Gee. I just heard you made $1 million. Where's your tax return?'"

Nelson says that too many Americans have not filed income taxes in Mexico even though they should. So far, the Mexican government has not taken much action on this issue. Expect that to change, he warns. Mexico is quickly upgrading its tax system and is likely to crack down. "There are probably about 5 to 10 years left of good times," Nelson estimates. He says the Mexican tax system is about as complex as the U.S. tax system but is less clearly defined.

Unlike the U.S. system, there are no case rulings to provide uniform interpretations of rules. As a result, there may be different interpretations, "depending upon who your Mexican accountant is and where you live."

Might it pay to give up your U.S. citizenship entirely? If taxes are lower in your new abode, it could. But Nelson suggests that if you do that because it benefits you financially, consider getting a ruling from the IRS that you're not giving it up to avoid U.S. taxes.

You should obtain this ruling, he says, if you have at least $100,000 in annual income and have a lot of assets. If you are renouncing your U.S. citizenship to avert taxes, you could be subject to stiff penalties.

Once you give up your U.S. citizenship, he adds, the United States has a policy of rarely giving it back. For more information on U.S. citizenship, see www.state.gov.

Consider starting a business in a new country even if you're retired; it could pay to have a small business in your foreign home, Nelson suggests. That's because, with a business, the IRS lets you exempt a certain amount of your income—$80,000 at this writing—each year on your U.S. tax return. Be sure to check the country's rules for setting up a business first, however. "One person I know who's doing it has a consulting business," Nelson says. "He operates totally on the phone from Mexico. He doesn't have to meet any clients. He takes a business trip up here once in a while. Yes, he can use this exclusion."

Be Careful About Real Estate

In Mexico, if a property is within 100 km (about 62 miles) of the ocean or in a federal district, as much of Mexico City is, a U.S. resident is prohibited from directly holding a title to property. The property, Nelson says, must be owned through a *Fideicomiso,* the only form of trust recognized by the Mexican government. It is created by a Mexican bank to hold property for the benefit of foreigners, he said.

Meanwhile, if you are the beneficiary of such a foreign trust or if you operate a business, the IRS requires you to file certain forms with your federal income tax. It can impose huge penalties if you don't. Also, title insurance only recently was introduced in Mexico. Yet, the process of buying a property operates similarly to the way it operates in the United States. "Always get title insurance," Nelson advises. If you can't, at least have an attorney or notary check the title. Be careful. (Without title insurance), your deeds are as good as the attorney or notary you hire." Too often, he says, people just buy property on contract and never have anything recorded: They're told, "That's the way we do things here." That can lead to trouble. Check the title and have a document showing that you own a property. Always have an escrow account. "Very few people have a mortgage because interest rates are prohibitive," observes Jeffrey D. Hill, a CFP with LPL Financial Services, Inc., in Denver. "Also, (mortgages) have variable rates."

Don't Neglect Car Insurance

An American going to Mexico with a car must have Mexican car insurance, Hill says. "U.S. car insurance typically does not cover an accident or anything else in Mexico." While Americans would be subject to the same laws as Mexicans if they have an accident, Hill says, they could find themselves facing added unforeseen problems. For example, he says, authorities could start investigating your immigration status.

Wills and Trusts

The good news is there is no estate tax in Mexico. However, U.S. citizens still are subject to U.S. estate taxes if assets in the inherited estate tally more than $1 million per person at this writing. Mexico doesn't recognize living trusts. "You can do a will or set up ownership of a piece of real estate so it goes to whoever you designate. The heir will have to get the title transfer and may pay fees and transfer tax," Nelson says.

Best Places to Retire Abroad

Here are the top 15 places to retire abroad, according to AARP's magazine, *Modern Maturity*. AARP, formerly the American Association of Retired Persons, sent researchers to 40 places worldwide. They graded each place using 12 categories, including weather, cost of living, affordable housing, cultural programs, health care, leisure, pollution, crime, transportation, political stability, health hazards, and access to technology:

1. Costa del Sol, Spain
2. Cinque Terre Italy
3. Provence, France
4. Bouquete, Panama
5. St. Vincent and the Grenadines
6. County Clare, Ireland
7. Nong Khai, Thailand
8. Crete, Greece
9. Ambergris Caye, Belize

10. Tunis, Tunisia
11. Algarve, Portugal
12. Cayman Islands
13. San Miguel de Allende, Mexico
14. Pafos, Cyprus
15. Ubid, Bali, Indonesia

Chapter 2

Thomas "Tom" Murphy: Sailing Away in Retirement

Thomas "Tom" Murphy, 65, had been retired for more than 10 years when we talked with him. His home is a 40-foot sailboat that he dubs *Monday Morning,* to mark the date—October 2, 1992—after which he no longer had to get up for work on Monday. Instead, he decided to take a $22,000 early retirement bonus to leave his job as a loading dock supervisor for the U.S. Postal Service. At 54, he was a year short of the minimum retirement age.

When we first talked with Tom, he was anchored off Boston in the dead of winter on his cell phone at a McDonald's restaurant near the Berklee College of Music. It was his tenth year living on a sailboat. Before his retirement, he had been earning close to $44,000 annually. Besides his $22,000 retirement bonus, he had some $50,000 to $60,000 in a thrift plan, more than $10,000 in IRAs, a few thousand dollars in the bank, and a $2,000 monthly income from a defined-benefit plan.

Before making the move onboard a boat 10 years ago, he had been renting an apartment with three others in Boston, paying $250 monthly. "I hated the idea of owning a place," he says. "I never liked it. I grew up in an apartment. My parents lived in apartments in Boston." His father had spent almost his entire career as an engineer on a fireboat, so Tom had grown up around the water. He had been on and off enough boats that he learned how to sail and had owned two boats before his retirement.

Tom says he has held back inflation by living on a boat. An apartment in Boston could cost him over $1,000 a month in this day and age. Likewise, a nice condo would cost him a good $500,000-plus in downtown Boston. The cost of his home today, he estimates, is no more than the $250-a-month rent he was paying a decade ago.

He doesn't necessarily travel to the most exotic locations. "I haven't even gone to the Bahamas," he says, noting that he much prefers cities. The places most people go in the Bahamas seem boring to him. Instead, he typically sails up and down the East Coast. He sails for a day at a time, stopping for extended periods (three or four months) mostly in larger cities. He carries a bicycle on his boat and often relies on public transportation. If he needs a car, he rents one.

Fortunately, Tom saved some for retirement. He began paying attention to his retirement savings in the mid-1980s. That's because the Civil Service retirement system was changing. A thrift savings plan was introduced. "Everybody at that point had to make an irrevocable decision to stay under the old plan or go with the new plan," he says. So he had to seriously think about his future. He decided to continue with the original defined-benefit plan, which fuels his retirement today, but he also decided to make voluntary contributions to the thrift savings plan. With the thrift plan, he could invest in mutual funds. "I couldn't take it off my taxes," he says. 'There was no government matching (contribution) or anything, but I still could put money in."

While working, he began living on the amount of money he figured he would need to live on during his retirement. The rest of his income went into the thrift savings plan.

Unfortunately, the thrift plan since has been liquidated, thanks to what he considers to be one of the greatest mistakes he made since living on a boat. When he bought his newer boat, a Freedom 40, he took out a ship's mortgage. In retrospect, he wishes he had paid off that mortgage before the bear market eradicated a good chunk of that money. "I think I lost about $50,000 by not paying (the mortgage) off right away," he said. "By the time I finished paying for it, all the mutual funds I was holding had dried up significantly."

His plan originally was to pay off the mortgage partially in 2000 and 2001 so he wouldn't get whacked for all the capital gains taxes in the same year. "But when 2001 came, scariness hit me. I left it, and it just kept diminishing in value. I really screwed that up."

When he left the post office, he first investigated the retiring in Costa Rica. At the time, the country was offering incentives to retirees. But the lifestyle was not for him. He had been some bicycle tours and thought about riding a bicycle to the coast California. He also had considered joining a crew on a boat. Then he noticed an article in *Cruising World* magazine detailing the expenses of living aboard.

"They actually used numbers," he says. "Some people spend hundreds of thousands of dollars. Some people spend $10,000. The ones spending $10,000 may or may not be happier than the others. But they did the article, and it dawned on me that I could actually afford it." He subsequently saw an ad for a 1971 30-foot Bristol sailboat and decided to pay cash for it—about $10,000. "It depends on what mood I'm in whether that sounds like a lot," he says. "It was a used car."

But he rationalized that if he bought the boat, it was a pretty safe bet that he'd be able to sell it at the same price. In fact, he says, when he sold it in 2000, his theory was proven correct— except for the fact that he had to pay a $2,000 commission to a broker. He expects, however, that the person who bought it from him will fix it up and sell it for $15,000 or $20,000. Sailboats, he explains, are in between cars and houses. Cars depreciate to the point that they're "worthless." "Houses appreciate even if they're worthless," he says. "Both hang in there if they're any good."

From 1993 until 1996, Tom's boat largely was stationary— with the exception of one-week trips now and then. By August 1996, he started cruising full-time. "I still have the last piece of rope I untied in the marina in Boston," he said. "It was a 60-foot piece of polypropylene rope."

The summer before he made that fateful move, his small pickup truck was involved in a head-on collision and his truck was totaled. The accident, he chuckles, saved him the trouble of having to sell his truck. Instead, the insurance company paid him.

Where Tom decides to settle his boat varies. "Normally I stay at anchor—out of choice and cheapness," he says. "If you drop anchor, you put a big hunk of iron down underneath the boat in the water," he explains. "You have nothing to do with anybody on shore. By contrast, in a marina your boat is tied up, and it can cost as much as $1 to $2 per

ing that marinas often charge by the length of
you can pay as much as $500 monthly.
ive at anchor," he says, "you need someplace
...da, the end of any street that runs down into
... acceptable place to tie a boat up. Often in such
... for free.
...nd marina managements have different attitudes about having liveaboards, which is what Tom is. "The town of North Palm Beach (Florida) doesn't want them there and has adopted ordinances," he notes. "The town of Palm Beach Gardens, Florida, doesn't care." At least one area on the west coast of Florida, he says, "forbids you to sleep on a boat, which is pretty ridiculous." And Georgia bans liveaboards altogether—yet, he says, there definitely are liveaboards in that state. "You can tell. They're the boats that have flower pots on the deck."

Inevitably, when a town adopts an ordinance aimed at getting rid of liveaboards, he says, it goes to court and eventually gets thrown out because navigation typically falls under federal jurisdiction.

***

In 2000, Tom moved up in the world. He spent $80,000 on his 1979 40-foot Freedom 40 sailboat. Not only was it roomier, but it also had a refrigerator and added the luxuries of an air-conditioner and a diesel heater. In the cold weather, he also uses an electric heater. There is a rug and built-in furniture. This is the new purveyor of the name *Monday Morning*. When we talked to Tom, his boat was docked in the marina in Boston at a cost of $2,000 for six months, including dockage. Had this been summer, he noted, the marina price would have been $6,000.

Tom says that his life is comfortable, thanks to the federal government's defined-benefit plan, which includes a cost-of-living allowance. At this writing, it was paying him close to $2,700 monthly. He was paying some $90 monthly for a pay-for-service Blue Cross/Blue Shield PPO-style health plan, one of at least 100 from which he is allowed to choose as a retirement benefit with the U.S. Postal Service. With his traveling, an HMO would be impractical.

In a few months, Tom expects to add the price of Medicare— $60 monthly—based on friends' recommendations that he carry both plans. His boat is paid off. He says he spends virtually all of his monthly income but still has some investments. Not long ago, he put about $25,000 in a Vanguard index fund. "The first week I went back in, it went up $1,000, and I said, 'Oh, my God. I did something right!'" he says. He also has $20,000 in bonds, $5,000 in an international index fund, and $20,000 in a money market fund.

His greatest expense is that he eats out a lot when he's docked—although generally not at expensive places. While sailing, he does his own cooking. "I haven't had a TV in 30 years," he says. "I read. I listen to the radio. It has nothing to do with boats. I'm just not much of a TV person. He says he prefers to read newspapers, science fiction, and publications such as *Scientific American.*

He spends about $800 annually for $75,000 worth of insurance for his boat. He saves an estimated $100 by picking up his cell phone each time he crosses the Florida line. It costs $900, he explains, to have Florida on his plan. His solution: As he sails to the Florida border, he calls his insurance company and directs it to add his Florida rider. As he heads back up north, upon hitting the Florida border, he calls again and tells the company to take off the rider. If he had sailed to the Bahamas, insurance would be even more expensive—$1,000 annually, he says.

He also saves money by doing his own maintenance work. "I can't afford to hire people," he says. "If I have a toilet backed up, I don't call the plumber. I will call someone for the engine— if I don't know what I'm doing. If I half know what I'm doing, I try to fix it myself."

Tom is not very worried about maintenance, though. He figures that a diesel engine, which costs about $9,000, would be his most costly expense. But those last a very, very long time. Unfortunately, he notes, the larger your boat is, the more things cost. For example, a sail on his 30-foot boat ran about $1,000, although he says he paid $650. On his newer boat, he figures that a sail would cost between $3,000 and $4,000. With his old boat, he was able to paint the bottom, a maintenance chore that needs to be done every two years, with just 2 gallons of paint. The paint he used ran about $100 to $130 a gallon.

On his newer boat, he needs at least 4 gallons to do the bottom. In addition, he estimates, it costs about $500 to haul the boat out of the water for the paint job and to put it back in. He views this maintenance as a household expense.

If he takes a longer trip, he brings along a crew. But the crew is made up of friends who volunteer. If he hired people, it would cost him a lot of money in addition to wages. "That would mean I would be in business, and I'd have trouble with the U.S. Coast Guard." Once you have a business or a boat over a certain size, he says, a license is required.

Tom admits there have been a few trying times on his boat. When he initially moved onto it, he spent the first week in Boston in below-freezing temperatures. He had to figure out how to heat the boat with an electric heater.

Then there was the thunderstorm that he'll never forget while traveling with a friend near the South Carolina-Georgia line. His friend woke him up. The two were 20 miles from shore. Lightning had started hitting very close. "I was watching lightning strikes to my left and to my right," he remembers. The greatest risk with storms, he says, is it can blow out all your electronics. Fortunately, this storm passed in about a half hour and no harm was done.

Normally, if there's a thunderstorm, he just anchors and waits it out. But for that particular storm, he simply was too far from shore. Then again, he says, his thunderstorm experience is not much different than if you were driving down the highway and something fell off a truck in front of you.

Tom likes heading north in hurricane season. "They never get hurricanes in Maine," he explains. "Hurricanes scare me." The last year a hurricane threatened, he says, he was in the Potomac, Maryland, area and didn't go into a marina. "I figured I was better off anchoring," he says, so he dropped four anchors and 300 feet of line on each one. The wind blew up to 50 knots. "I was very impressed with the marina." he says. They came down and told everybody in anchorage to go into the marina."

He figured that if the boat were tied up in a marina, it would get bashed. He did go ashore for a while, but the hurricane never actually hit.

When Tom travels, he sometimes finds friends to come along. Once he had a friend join him in Stuart, Florida, for a while. Another joined him in Brunswick, Georgia, and stayed until he reached Virginia.

But there is also a lot of fellowship among people who live on their boats and travel the seas. He says that the liveaboard community represents a unique culture unto itself.

"The other liveaboard cruisers are a wonderful set of people," he says. For example, in 2001, Tom spent one of his more pleasant New Year's Eves in Biscayne Bay with seven people. There were two Canadian boats, an English boat, and his. "Seven of us were on one boat. The one whose boat we were on was a gourmet cook. He reached into the galley and pulled something unbelievable out of the oven every 15 minutes."

One of the people was a retired superintendent with the British police in Scotland Yard. "I'm not apt to meet anybody like that," Tom says. "We get along fine. There tends to be (a lesser) class distinction if you're all in the same boat. Somebody who has a very expensive boat is obviously rich, and somebody who has a poor boat is obviously poor, but they get along fine. If they're liveaboards, they see each other as liveaboards. There's a mutual sense of respect—despite the fact that one might make $12,000 a year and another $12,000 a month."

Despite the risks, Tom says the pleasures of sailing are very simple. Take the time he was sailing down Hawk Channel between Miami and Marathon, Florida, last year with a friend from Boston. "The wind was light, at about 10 knots," he says, "but the water was smooth and the boat drove easily through it. The water looked like clear green glass. You could see the ground 12 feet down perfectly. We saw some dolphins come by the boat and take up station at our bow. I walked forward and looked down at them. There were four adults and one small one—I guess a juvenile. We watched them while they stayed with us for about 15 minutes. They watched us, too. The water was so clear and smooth that we could see their every move."

Another time that Tom will never forget is traveling on the intracoastals, being anchored in the middle of marshes in Georgia, with no one around for 20 miles and birds screeching.

"You're not driving up and down I-95 and going into little shopping centers," he explains. "You're going into small towns in the Carolinas. The scenery is being out in the open."

Tom says he lucked into his 10-year-old lifestyle. "I went into it cautiously. I went into it cheaply to see if I actually did like it. Compared with a house, my cabin is kind of small," he says, "but the backyard is unbelievable!"

When traveling, Tom normally gets up at sunrise and goes to bed at 9 P.M. "When I'm in the city, I tend to stay up later than I should. Today (a Sunday), I didn't get up until 8 A.M."

He admits that this year he made a major mistake—staying in Boston for the below-freezing winter. It was a fluke. "I like being in cities," he says. "I was getting ready to leave, but I put off leaving. It got to be the middle of October, and there were three northeast storms coming through and I waited. After that, it was almost November. I wasn't going to travel then. I'd still be in the Carolinas in the beginning of December!"

By our second interview with him, in the dead of winter, he had left his boat in Boston and taken a flight to Florida, where he was staying with friends in Miami Beach. He was planning to rent a car and drive to Florida's west coast before flying back to Boston about two weeks later. It was unusual for him to fly. More commonly, he stays south of Maryland and takes a train from Baltimore to and from Boston. But his mother, in Boston, was in failing health. He typically travels away from his boat once every year or two. In fact, he says he has been outside the Eastern Standard Time zone just three times in his life—visiting Jerusalem, Nova Scotia, and Costa Rica. When we talked to him, he envisioned leaving Boston around the spring for Maine.

Tom says he carries a credit card and two ATM cards. He leaves one ATM card at home in case he loses his wallet. He pays off his credit cards by having payments automatically debited from his credit union checking account. "I'm kind of thinking about looking into online banks, but I haven't spent any time looking at them," he says. "Credit unions are trustworthy. They're nonprofit and member owned.

"I don't live on credit cards. I don't carry a balance," he stresses. However, he pays for most of his transactions with them rather than carrying cash. "I'm the guy in the drug store who spends $1.08 on a credit card," he says. That, he explains, is just enough to beat the 99-cent minimum charge that the drug store sets. He has his retirement check sent to his checking account monthly. "Staying (in Boston) in the winter, I spent more money on clothes than in the first five years.

I normally live in flip-flops, so my high expenses for shoes are $10 for shoes every six months."

Tom is a walking encyclopedia of ways to avoid ATM surcharges. Those are the fees charged to nonbank customers at ATMs—over and above the charges levied by your own bank on your ATM card. Publix Supermarkets throughout Florida have no surcharges. "Publix gets all my business," he says. Credit unions tend not to charge. Here in Boston, there's a system that little banks have called SUM, where you don't have to pay surcharges." The SUM Program, administered by the NYCE Network, has more than 440 financial institutions and 2,800 ATMs participating.

While many who travel have mail sent to a friend or relative to be forwarded, Tom has opted to have a service in Islamorada, Florida, pack up his mail periodically and ship it, minus the junk mail, to whatever address he wants. The cost is $199 a year plus postage. His mail almost always fits into a priority mail envelope, he says. Sometimes he has it shipped via UPS or Federal Express to a marina.

He also votes. "The clerk in the city of Boston is very laissez faire," he says, noting that the reaction might be different in places such as Florida, which had election problems in 2000. "I told the clerk I'm living on a boat. He said just to use (my) last address. I ended up using my mother's address in Boston, and we just sold her house, so I figured I'd just dot the Fs and cross the T's. I belong to a yacht club, so I changed the domicile to the yacht club address." Fortunately, he says, he does not need to worry about state income taxes because he already paid them while working as a federal employee.

He has a computer, which he runs off his cell phone. "It's like sucking through a straw," he says. "If you turn off all the pictures on the Internet, things go much faster."

Tom says the two greatest concerns he had about his retirement were his health benefits and the formula that would determine his cost-of-living increases. Although his current income is "nothing to jump and scream about," it is covering his expenses.

Anybody considering retirement on a boat should not think about it too hard, Tom advises. "If you read all the magazine articles about what to do, you can get paralyzed with fear about doing the wrong thing. You make mistakes, but none of them is going to be fatal."

He also says that nothing has to be terribly dangerous financially. Although there is a great deal of talk in newsgroups about how much it costs to live on a boat, it really depends upon the individual.

"Some people would never consider staying at anchor, but they stay in a marina every night and pay f 100 to $150 a day just for marina fees," he says. "Some wouldn't go into a marina if their life depended on it. You can't generalize. It depends on what style of living you want. There are some people who work at McDonald's, and that's it."

The only mistake he says he made is not paying off his boat before the market tanked. "You can get a decent boat in the range of $50,000," he says. Houseboats tend to be the cheapest, and you can find one for $25,000 to $75,000. "When you buy a boat, you always have it surveyed. That's the equivalent of a home inspection." In addition, if you live on a boat, interest on a boat mortgage, just like a home mortgage, is tax deductible.

Doing It Yourself

Living on a boat can be a lower-cost, romantic way to spend your retirement. Imagine spending the summers in Maine and the winters in the Caribbean Islands!

However, over the last few years, according to experts, there has been a national rise in efforts to get rid of liveaboards. "From my perspective, there are two motivating factors," says Richard M. Stephens, a land use regulations attorney in Bellevue, Washington. "One is purely economic." People who own waterfront homes or property don't want other people living on the water. The second reason is environmental. "They want to make sure people living on a boat have adequate sanitation facilities."

Andrew J. Goldstein, a Newark, New Jersey, attorney specializing in maritime law, advises that you carefully consider environmental issues. 'You can't just dump your sewage or oil over the side." Plus, you need to follow "the rules of the road," which in the United States are administered by the U.S. Coast Guard.

"When there's a collision, usually one of the vessels did not follow the rules of the road," Goldstein says. Also, even though states typically require that you have insurance for your car, they don't necessarily require it for a boat. Nevertheless, it's important to have some.

The U.S. Coast Guard warns that if you're anchoring, you are prohibited from impeding navigation. You can't just anchor in the middle of the channel. The U.S. Coast Guard designates special anchorage areas, at the request of the local harbor master. There also are special rules for anchoring, largely aimed at boats that are at least 65 feet. Plus, you are required to carry things such as life jackets and flares on your boat.

Experts say that if you're considering living on a boat, you need to carefully check out regulations administered by the U.S. Coast Guard, as well as state and local regulations. All can vary dramatically.

You need to watch your registration—particularly if you're staying in different areas for long periods. In New Jersey, for example, vessels must be registered with the director of motor vehicles, notes Goldstein. "If you're going to register with Delaware, you can't bring (your boat) into New Jersey and keep it indefinitely. Each state will allow you to keep a vessel for a certain period of time before they want their own revenues."

Living on a Boat Can Be Cheap

The cost of living on a houseboat, motor boat, or sailboat is estimated to be about the same as the cost of renting. However, living on a boat in expensive metropolitan areas may be cheaper than renting an apartment. The cost often depends on the style and size of the boat and where it is kept. You can buy boats that are the equivalent to one- or two-bedroom apartments, and then some houseboats are like mansions.

You have to consider several costs when purchasing a boat. Among them:

- Boat survey (inspection) fee. This one-time inspection, can run from $200 to more than $3,000. It is based on the size of the boat.
- Boat insurance, which is similar to car insurance. Its price depends on the types of coverage you select and such factors as the boat's size, type, age, and location. Because boats typically cost more than cars, expect it to be more expensive than what you would pay for a car, experts say.
- Fuel.

- Marina docking fees, which can run upward of $50 to $150 per day.
- Liveaboard or extra utility charges of $25 a month or more, depending on the marina.
- Annual lease fee at a boat slip, which can cost some $3,000 a year or more. You also might lease a slip seasonally.

If you're thinking about living on a boat, Tom suggests that you look at boating magazines, such as *Living Aboard,* the online magazine at www.livingaboard.com; *Liveaboard Magazine;* and *Cruising World.* "When you look at national magazines, keep in mind that things don't necessarily cost as much as you see. If you go to boat shows, you're going to see nothing but expensive new boats. The dynamics of boat shows are, they can't afford to show anything that isn't expensive because the fees for boat shows are enormous. Look around in boat yards. I'm in a sailboat, but there are people who have trawler yachts—which is a big, slow boat—not much faster than sailboats." They have much more room in them than on a normal sailboat. "I thought about a trawler, but I like sailing—without the engine running."

Tor Pinney, author of *Ready for Sea! How to Outfit the Modern Cruising Sailboat* (Sheridan House, 2002), says that to live comfortably on a boat, you probably need one between 30 and 60 feet long. Once you go longer than that, he says, expect to incur the added expense of hiring crew.

"What is a reasonable boat to live on," he says, "depends on what a person needs to be comfortable, the budget, and the intended use." Regardless of the type of boat you select, he says, you can expect to pay anywhere from $30,000 up to $1 million.

Houseboats, which are used for calm bodies of water, have wide beams and cabins that cover most of the deck. Inside are private staterooms, a shower, a galley, and an eating and entertainment area. They can be one or two stories, Pinney says, and often are box-shaped, with large outdoor areas on roof sundecks. They don't need to be provided with as much power as other types of boats, which taper toward the bow to a point.

Trawlers, for large rivers, lakes, and oceans on moderate days, sit high on the water. They may come with a big cabin, a bathroom, a galley, and an eating and entertainment center. The boats are suited for cruising long distances in the intra-coastal waterways of the United States and the Great Lakes. "If you want to go voyaging, but want to take it easy, trawler type vessels have become more popular in the last decade," Pinney says. "They're not particularly fast, but they're strong, comfortable, and secure. Some trawlers are capable of crossing oceans. Others are not. It has to do with the construction and size." Larger trawlers, he notes, are often called, "expedition yachts."

Cruising sailboats, which are used to sail in the ocean off-coast, also may have cabins, bathrooms, galleys, and eating and entertainment areas. "They're designed and built for ocean sailing," Pinney says. "With them, you can cross oceans without having to carry enormous amounts of fuel. The motor is auxiliary on a sailboat. It helps you get in and out of places. You plan most of your voyaging to be propelled by sails. It's quieter too."

You can do some living and traveling on catamarans, which have two hulls, or trimarans, which have three hulls. They typically are good for cruising and anchoring in shallow waters. Large catamarans may come with cabins and other facilities. "If you're going to live at dock, a houseboat's the way to go," Pinney says. "You get the most room for the least amount of money. As soon as you want to start traveling with the boat outside of a bay or river, then most will choose a trawler or cruising sailboat."

Chapter 3

Herman "Gene" Liberman: Dancing Around the World

Herman "Gene" Liberman perpetually has a smile on his face, despite the fact that he retired at age 62 with a relatively small amount of savings. A lifelong bachelor, he hung up his spikes in 1983 from his job as an insurance salesman with just $64,000 to his name. Now 82 years old, Gene has a kitty that has been ravaged by investments in technology mutual funds, which lost more than 70 percent of their value between March 2000 and September 2002. Even so, he's not worried. He calculates that his monthly expenses represent only about 55 percent of his monthly income, so he has plenty of money left over.

Upon retirement, Gene finally was able to realize the type of life he had always dreamt of—on his own terms. His lifelong love of dancing put him in demand as a dance host. In fact, that sideline skill is just one reason he has been able to lay claim to 32 cruises since he retired. He never had the opportunity to travel while he worked.

"I've traveled transatlantic and I went through the Mediterranean," he says. "I've been to Greece, Egypt, Turkey, Israel, the Black Sea countries, and also Romania. I went to the Ukraine and Bulgaria. I went on the Amazon from Fort Lauderdale for 27 days and the heart of the Amazon to Manus."

You might think that this world traveler has quite a bit of money. His apartment complex is richly landscaped with palm trees and other indigenous Florida vegetation, carrying the look of an exclusive country club. His immaculate Mediterranean-style luxury one-bedroom apartment, complete with a washer and dryer, comes with a whirlpool, swimming pool, and clubhouse, and it overlooks a lake.

However, Gene scoffs at the retirement gurus who say you need more than $1 million to retire comfortably today. 'You need that if you want a yacht and you want to live on the ocean," he says. "It's according to the lifestyle you want. "I've always lived within my means. I do use credit cards. But I never run up a credit card with more than I think I can pay off within a short time."

Although Gene always looks for bargains, he has been able to retire so comfortably with such limited resources for several other reasons. While some strategies came by happenstance— just by following his heart—others involved seeing an opportunity and grabbing it.

For one thing, he lives in Boynton Beach, Florida, and Florida has no state income tax. Although Gene rented apartments his whole life, he always loved Florida. He vacationed there steadily between 1975 and 1979 and decided that the lifestyle was for him. Before his retirement, he put down 20 percent on a furnished two-bedroom, two-bath condominium that he bought for $35,000 in Boynton Beach and rented it out—for $400 monthly. Meanwhile, he continued working as an insurance agent in White Plains, New York. He subsequently rented the condo in January, February, and March, getting $600 monthly for those three months. Upon his retirement, he moved into that condo. Not only was his cost of living lower, but with his move, he never needed to pay a state income tax again.

Gene does not drive. That saves him not only the expense of a car, but also the costs of repairs, gas, and car insurance. Born in Newark, New Jersey, Gene had obtained a driver's license. But he found that while living in the New York area he did not need it due to the region's excellent public transportation.

Upon moving to Florida, he obtained a Florida driver's license. "It made me too nervous to drive," he says. "I let it lapse."

Fortunately, many of his friends who are also retired have cars. "Sometimes if a friend is going shopping, he will ask me if I want to go along," he says. Gene's apartment also is fairly close to two supermarkets. In cooler weather, he enjoys walking.

Despite all its luxuries, Gene's current apartment building actually is federally subsidized housing, restricted to senior citizens on limited incomes. As a result, Gene's rent is controlled. At this writing, he paid just $514 monthly, plus electricity and water, compared with other area rents averaging $750 for less luxurious apartments. And although his building is limited to senior citizens, other luxury buildings on the same grounds have no age restrictions, so he is not completely isolated. Strip shopping centers are situated directly across the major highway from his apartment.

While living in his villa, Gene read in a senior's newspaper that directly across the street, a seniors' building was under construction for persons at least 62 years old. "It sounded like it was going to be nice," he says, so he walked across the street and registered for a unit. At the time, he says, there was an income ceiling. A single person could not earn more than $14,000 annually. For a married couple, he said, the threshold was $18,000. "I was the second person to move in 1990.

"Every year, they check my income. I show them all the checks I get. They ask that I show them a bank statement. They don't ask how much I have in mutual funds or stocks."

He slashes medical costs by belonging to a health maintenance organization (HMO). "Fortunately, I've always been in good health," he says, "so my expenses were very minimal.

I have never been hospitalized in my life!" Gene doesn't smoke and drinks only in moderation. In fact, "everything in moderation" is his credo. He rarely eats desserts. His employer continued his private medical insurance from the point when he retired until he was able to qualify for Medicare. Gene joined the Humana Gold Plus plan in 1988. Under the program, Medicare pays the HMO. 'The only premium I pay is what is deducted for Medicare each month. Right now, it's just $59 a month.

"I've always been fortunate in that I've had good care," Gene says. When he had a hernia operation, conducted as an outpatient procedure, he paid nothing. "If I go to a specialist, it costs $30. I'm allowed $150 for eye exams and glasses. If you get generic medication, it's only $10. I happen to be able to take generic."

All except one of his friends is retired. "Some go to the same (doctor's) office I do," he says, "so it's very convenient." Often they drive. He actually had walked to the office until recently, when his doctors' office moved farther away from his home.

One of Gene's chief joys in retirement has been his first love since childhood: dancing. As a child growing up in Bound Brook, New Jersey, he often went to the movies. After each movie, there generally were about five vaudeville acts. "Those were live. There was no television, just radio," he says. "When I came home, I used to try to imitate everything I saw. My mother saw I had a talent."

However, life at home was tough. "We weren't on welfare, but we didn't have any money. We had a house when I was a child around the Depression. We lost the house in Bound Brook. We had to move into an apartment." Gene's late father, who owned a news and tobacco store, worked 6 A.M. to 11 P.M. The family had to fill in while his father took a nap in the afternoon or when he was ill. "We had to open up and close."

Gene took refuge in his dancing. He began to take tap dance lessons. "I used to love Fred Astaire, Gene Kelly, and Donald O'Connor."

He graduated from Bound Brook High School in New Jersey and began working for Pathe Film, a company that processed feature films.

Upon entering the U.S. Air Force in 1942, he was disqualified from fighting due to an eye impediment. That opportunity helped pave the way for his passion later in life. Vaudeville had begun to lose popularity in the 1940s when Gene volunteered for the "Special Services" or entertainment unit.

Gene spent most of his time in Gowen Field, near Boise, Idaho. He had regular working hours but often was excused for rehearsals. He began performing in a number of shows. Generally, they were variety shows on the base or for charities, and Gene tap-danced—often solo. One of the shows, "The Gowen Field Frolics," was a minstrel show. "I just did my tap dancing number," he says. The late actor Jimmy Stewart, who was a captain in the service at the time, attended that show at his base. "He came backstage to congratulate everyone," Gene says.

One newspaper account even quoted the famous actor as saying, "The show was one of the very best I've ever had an opportunity of seeing."

Gene always wanted to get into show business but never pursued it. After leaving the service as a sergeant, he became a dance teacher.

He had attended the Arthur Murray dance studio in New York, under the GI Bill.

He once tried out for the chorus in a Broadway show. "It was called 'Follow the Girls,'" he says, "starring Gertrude Niesen. I had a contact that got me an interview to replace one of the men in the chorus. I did fine when I was tested at the Broad-hurst Theatre in Manhattan. But I was told later that the only reason I did not get the job was because in the 1940s, after I got out of the service, all the boys and girls in choruses had to be the same height. I'm only 5-foot-7. The person leaving was very much taller, and I would not be able to fit into the chorus line. Also at that time, they began to incorporate a lot of ballet into the chorus numbers, and I did not have any training in ballet. So I didn't pursue it anymore."

He decided instead to follow a more practical career course. After his six-month stint as a dancing teacher, he took several jobs as a bookkeeper or office manager. His last stop: an insurance agency. He started doing office work there but eventually attended insurance school and obtained his New York State insurance license. That final career lasted 24 years.

Gene rarely got a raise and never made more than $30,000 annually, including commissions. But fortunately, he did something that many might never have even considered. He asked his boss and his partner about setting up a retirement plan. They agreed and matched 15 percent of his annual salary. They also started an annuity for him. That stash largely served as Gene's ticket to a comfortable retirement in Florida. He saved less than 10 percent of his retirement monies on his own.

Gene first became a dance host in 1986—three years after moving to Florida. A widow who lived in his condominium complex had been a student at a dance studio in Delray Beach and invited him to a dinner and dance competition at an area country club. "They needed men to dance with the women who were students," he says. "When the people who ran the studio saw how I danced, they asked if I would be interested in coming to their parties every Tuesday night." The deal: He was paid $25 to dance with the women who took lessons for two hours. Later he earned $30.

He participated in those parties for 14 years and subsequently began attending similar events at area retirement homes.

"I felt great about, it!" he says of his initial reaction to his new gig. What was not to like? Often there was an open bar and live music. He didn't have to pay for wine, liquor, or soda. On the table were pretzels or potato chips. At Christmas and Thanksgiving, there were catered dinners at the studio.

"At first, I loved to dance. You met a lot of wonderful people, and you became just one big happy family."

However, as time progressed, his arthritis started to bother him. When you're paid to host a party, you're required to dance constantly. "We could not sit around," he says. "When the music played, you got up. The only time you didn't dance was if there were too many men." Those times were rare.

Gene never once pauses to jog his memory. The details come vividly pouring out. He explains how he landed such a plum job as a dance host on a cruise ship. When reading a newspaper, he noticed an article about dance hosts on cruise ships. "They were using men on certain lines to dance with single women on cruise ships. I inquired and got an answer."

Gene had responded to an ad and was contacted by an agent in 1992. Under the setup, he paid the agent $29 per day. In exchange, the cruises were free, except for about another $5 daily in tips.

"I had passenger and cruise status," he reports. "We dined with passengers in the evening. I had all the advantages of being a passenger."

Depending upon room availability, he either shared a room or was provided with his own.

"The only drawback is, that some days, you may not feel like dancing," he admits. "Or, you may have some people who are very difficult to dance with, but you still have to put on a smile and you have to do it. Yet, it really is very nice for anyone who wants to go and see the world and not spend a lot of money."

Gene says he has been very lucky. The trips he obtained as a dance host were to places that he would not likely have spent the money to go to on his own.

Today Gene lives comfortably on $1,206 monthly, including $868 monthly in Social Security. To this day, he laughs over his annuity, which turned out to be an attractive investment for him. When it came time to retire, he had the option of cashing out his annuity and investing the proceeds, or "annuitizing" and getting monthly payments for life. He opted to annuitize. He selected an arrangement called "10-year period certain." Under such a plan, he gets monthly payments for life. If he dies within the first 10 years of annuitizing, the proceeds of the annuity go to his beneficiary. If he lives longer than 10 years, the insurance company keeps the proceeds of his investment when he dies.

Many said that Gene was foolish to annuitize. He would have been better off taking the lump sum and investing it, they argued. Well, they were wrong. "I've been collecting $212.50 a month for 19 years!" Gene says. That tallies nearly $48,500— significantly more than the $22,000 or so that had been in the annuity when he retired at age 62. As many of his friends struggled with lost monthly income due to a bear market and federally insured interest rates dipping below 3 percent, Gene has peace of mind. He knows that those same guaranteed monthly payments will continue for as long as he lives.

Each day, Gene walks 30 minutes without stopping between 8 A.M. and 9 A.M. "Then I do some reading and watch some TV. Maybe two or three times a week, I go out to lunch with retired friends." On weekends, he helps out a friend in his business by doing office work, picking up some extra entertainment expenses in exchange.

"I'm a coupon clipper and I watch all the specials when I go out shopping," he says. "Also, I'm a thrift shop person. I don't usually pay full price for anything. I'm a person who looks for sales on clothing, food, anything."

Gene uses his credit cards to have a good time. But he pays them off. He doesn't let the balances get out of hand. The largest balance Gene has ever carried came shortly after he retired, he says: He had charged $4,000. He solved that simply by going to work part time. First he worked a few months for an insurance agency and later worked a year and a half in a video rental store, when he paid off the debt.

He sometimes charges cruises when he sees a great deal. Then when he does make credit card payments, it generally is in large amounts. He never pays just the minimum monthly required balance. "I pay $300 to $400 a month," he says. At this writing, his balance was slightly higher than he would like— about $1,800, he acknowledges. So, he has made the supreme sacrifice. He has taken a short break from his traveling.

Gene admits that he hasn't necessarily been the best investor. Nevertheless, that hasn't dampened his ability to enjoy retirement. When he sold his first condo in Florida, he made just a $3,000 profit, he says, but had put $7,500 into it. "I lost money." Then in 1986, he bought a patio home for $62,000 and had a mortgage at 9.50 percent before selling it some four years later for $72,000. He had put $6,000 into it.

Often financial planners say that the most difficult year of retirement is the first. Not for Gene, who initially enjoyed sleeping late every day.

"That was just the most wonderful period of my life," he laughs. "I didn't have to adjust. It took me a day or two."

Of course, not everyone has the same perspective, he admits. "Everyone is different when it comes to retirement. There are some people who are not happy because they don't know what to do with themselves. I have never had a problem wondering what to do during the day. I enjoy my own company. I don't mind eating alone. I love to read. I love to look at television. I love to go out shopping or to visit somebody. Some people don't want to socialize. They don't want to do anything.

"Some people are not happy retired, and some people, I've read, have had to go back to work when they thought they'd never have to go back.

"I don't have that problem. I've had people say to me my whole life, 'I don't know how you do it.' I don't know how I do it, either. I have an innate sense of what I should do and what I shouldn't do. I know the value of things, and I watch what I spend.

"Some people are always spending money—more than what's coming in. They're always in trouble. You have people with $50,000 in credit card debt."

For anyone who would like to retire, Gene advises putting as much as is allowed into an IRA, if they can afford it. "If you're going to get a job, always try to get a job that has some sort of pension plan and health benefits," he adds. "Most of my life, I worked where there were no benefits."

Gene suggests that if you lack money, you might investigate lower-cost areas of the country like he did. "I investigated Florida because I was invited as a guest by someone who had a condo in Florida."

Of course, you also have to figure out whether you have enough money to live on. He had to wait until he was 62 to retire, he says, because he simply didn't have enough money to retire earlier.

Not long ago, Gene showed us a video taken of him on a cruise talent show. At age 79, he was doing a soft-shoe. At least twice, he explains, he was invited to participate on ships' talent revues. There were no winners, he says—just gifts for all participants. He also participated in two professional revues. "Two different cruise directors on separate cruises never saw me dance, but they took my word for it and put me on. I loved it!" When he dances, many of the passengers have a very hard time believing his age.

That, he says, is the closest he ever got to Broadway.

Doing It Yourself

Like Gene Liberman, you might be able to cut your cost of living considerably in retirement if you can live without a car. The American Automobile Association calculates that the annual cost of owning and operating a new car averages $7,754. That includes gas and oil, maintenance, tires, insurance, depreciation, license, registration, taxes, and the finance charge on your loan. It assumes that you drive 15,000 miles annually. In fact, you can calculate the cost based on your own car usage by visiting www.aaasouth.com/auto_cost_calculator.asp.

Although you might pay less for a used car, the City of Detroit Consumer Affairs Department notes that a used vehicle often requires you to "sink hundreds of dollars into repairs shortly after purchasing it." By contrast, it reports, an unlimited monthly bus pass through the Detroit Department of Transportation costs under $50, or less than $600 annually.

You also can save a bundle by relocating to an area that has low taxes. According to the newsletter, Bottom Line Personal, "South Dakota and Tennessee have the lowest overall tax burden ... followed closely by Florida and Texas." States that had no personal income tax at this writing include Alaska, Florida, Nevada, South Dakota, Texas, Washington, and Wyoming. For more specific information on taxes, visit www.taxsites.com.

Finding Low-Cost Places to Live

Don't expect to have the luck of Gene Liberman when it comes to finding subsidized housing when you retire, says Andrew Kochera, senior policy adviser for AARP, formerly the American Association of Retired Persons, in Washington D.C. "Ads would be unusual. In most places, there are very low vacancy rates, so it's not necessary to advertise." If anything, there often are waiting lists for government-subsidized low-rent apartments. Any ads, he suggests, are most apt to be running in rural areas.

But just because no one is advertising to charge you below-market rent doesn't mean you should not do your own leg work, Kochera stresses. AARP estimates that there are 1.7 million renter households headed by someone age 62 and older who live in some kind of federally subsidized housing. That does not include vacant apartments. Nor does it include all the state-subsidized, locally subsidized, or privately run programs. It also omits all the programs that require you to be just 55 years old and those that set no age restrictions whatsoever.

"It is really a morass of programs that are out there," Kochera says, noting that no central database for subsidized housing currently exists.

Kochera suggests that if you're looking for a low-rent apartment, first contact these agencies:

- Your area's public housing authority. Don't know the name of the agency? Consider contacting your town council or governing body to ask. Frequently, the agency has "public housing authority" in its name, he says. The exact role of housing agencies varies by area, he warns. Sometimes they maintain waiting lists for properties, and sometimes they don't. "At the very least, they should be able to refer you to properties where they don't maintain waiting lists."
- Your state's housing finance agency. This agency may be able to give you the scoop on whether any developers have applied to build subsidized housing that ultimately could offer low rents in your area. It also might have information on other subsidized programs. To track down a contact for your state housing finance agency, visit the National

Council of State Housing Finance Agencies at www.ncsha.org. Click on About NCSHA and then click on Members.
- Your area's agency on aging. This agency also should be able to refer you to low-rent or low-cost housing programs available. To track down an area office on aging near you, you can visit www.aoa.gov.

When you call these agencies, make certain you do some probing. Before providing any information on your income, first ask generally what the age and income restrictions are for any program that might be available. Don't think you'll qualify? Be absolutely sure to ferret out all the other programs that might be available in your area. For example, if you don't qualify for a federally assisted program, specifically ask whether there might be any other state, local, or private programs available.

If the person you've contacted does not know, ask to be referred to someone who does.

"The real key for rental housing is going to be the income level," Kochera says. However, these requirements differ substantially. The U.S. Department of Housing and Urban Development has certain kinds of rental programs with one set of rules. Low-income tax credit programs may have different rules and income qualifications, and locally subsidized programs might have yet another set of rules.

If you absolutely can't qualify for any low-rent programs in your area, Kochera suggests that you visit www.realtor.com and click on Apartments and Rentals. You might be able to find rentals that meet your qualifications. Also, certain real estate agencies specialize in finding low-rent apartments for those who can't qualify for government assistance. You may be able to find these agencies via ads in rental magazines available for free on racks in local supermarkets and drug stores.

Another factor to consider in cutting your rent may be rent-controlled apartments. Rent control exists in California; District of Columbia; Tacoma Park, Maryland; New Jersey; and New York, according to the National Multi-Housing Council. "Rent control regulations literally differ from city to city," Kochera says. "There is no standard form of rent control."

Just because a local area permits rent control does not mean that there will be any rent-controlled apartments available, he says. Often persons in rent-controlled apartments can't leave because market rents would be too high. If an apartment does become available, chances are good that you won't be paying what the previous resident is paying anyway. Once these units become available again, Kochera says, the rents often revert to market levels, or they may be subject to new regulations that often mean higher rents.

Nevertheless, it doesn't hurt to call either the office of the city council or the local office responsible for overseeing enforcement of rent control.

Looking for a low-cost loan for your home? Kochera suggests that you try for a Federal Housing Authority loan or, if you qualify, a Veteran's Administration loan. Your best bet, he says, might be to track down a mortgage broker that specializes in these types of loans. Or visit www.hud.gov or www.homeloans.va.gov.

Cruising for Free

Who wouldn't like to provide a skill in exchange for a free cruise? Mark Landon, owner of Shipsjobs.com and publisher of the book, *Cruise Ship Crews,* suggests that you might be able to do this by contacting the cruise ship's director of entertainment. On smaller ships that may not have an entertainment director, try the ship's hotel director.

"Most people make the mistake of sending it to the director of human resources," he says. "That's a complete waste of time."

Yes, Landon says, there are opportunities for dance hosts, sometimes called ambassador hosts, and guest lecturers.

"Dance hosts not only dance, but they participate in activities and socialize," he says. "Lectures consist of anything topical that the company feels passengers could relate to." Health and arts and crafts are in great demand, he says. Politics and financial planning are not.

Landon suggests that, if possible, you send a videotape, a letter, a bio, and a synopsis of your material, if you're lecturing. If you don't have a videotape, an 8-inch-by-10-inch head shot will work. The best opportunities for such plum jobs are apt to be on the five-star lines—Crystal, Cunard, Silversea, Radisson Seven Seas, and Seabourn. Lectures, he says, are provided only when the ship is at sea—not when the ship is in port. "Five-star ships tend to have more sea days because they move around the world."

Other perks for dance hosts and lecturers might include drink allowances. Lecturers and dance hosts may be provided with extra money to buy passengers drinks. While on land, employees also may escort bus tours, which otherwise may cost thousands of dollars. A dance host or lecturer's primary responsibility on a tour bus would be to count passengers, help out, and socialize.

For retirees considering becoming a cruise ship dance host or lecturer, Landon advises the following:

- Verify all costs of a cruise. If they tell you that you're going to get a free cruise, find out how much airfare will be. Sometimes airfare is not covered.
- Ask whether you may bring a spouse. Gentlemen dance hosts typically can't.
- Ask about port taxes. "Some of the ships say your cruise is free, but you have to pay port taxes."
- Don't assume that a free cruise is totally free. You proba bly have to pay tips to the cabin steward, waiter, busboy, and bartenders.

Even though it might not be in writing, he adds, you're expected to socialize. In fact, whether you're brought back on the ship could well be determined by the amount of socializing you do.

Chapter 4

Duane and Dolores "Dee" Mark: Building Their Dream Retirement Home

The Marks, of Golden Valley, Arizona, might be living evidence that it's never too late to have retirement dreams—even if you're in debt.

Dolores "Dee" Mark, 65, retired from a career as a waitress and restaurant manager about eight years ago- before she remarried in 1996. She wanted to spend more time with her new husband, Duane, who is 62. Now she spends her days cooking, working on crafts, and driving nails with her husband on what the two anticipate will be their dream retirement home. It will be an energy-efficient southwestern stucco Diablo-style home with an observation deck above the master bedroom. The property has a breathtaking view overlooking the Black Mountains, just 20 miles west of Kingman, Arizona.

Duane, a carpenter, laughs at financial planners' suggestions that you need $1 million or more to retire. When we talked with the couple, they had $14,000 in credit card debt. In addition, they owed about $1,500 more on the 2.5 acres they bought. The couple currently sleeps in a 30-foot trailer that attaches to their pickup truck.

Duane's goal is very simple: He'd like to live his retirement years in their new home with no debt. He anticipates that the two can live very comfortably on close to $1,200 monthly in Social Security, plus perhaps, another $10,000 annually that he expects to bring in through odd jobs or an occasional published magazine article. He figures that he will reach his goal of living debt-free in a completely self-contained house in a little over three years—by age 65. By that time, due to a carefully thought-out home design, his only ongoing monthly expenses should be a small propane bill and telephone bill.

Neither spouse was a stranger to hardship before the fateful day when Duane offered to help Dee do the dishes at a Toledo, Ohio, unity church spaghetti dinner.

With 23 years in the restaurant business, Dee had been raising her three daughters on her own after getting divorced from her husband in 1972. "We had two restaurants and lost one to (my husband's) gambling debt," she says. Then in 1979, Dee was diagnosed with cervical cancer and needed a hysterectomy. She had no medical insurance. After her illness, she opened a catering business for one year, but she didn't have enough money to keep it going, so she closed it. She worked both in management and as a waitress in several restaurants.

Meanwhile, Duane, with two children and a 14-employee contracting business in Ohio, lost his business, home, and retirement savings after he needed major surgery. Just before he was diagnosed with ulcerated colitis, business had slowed. "I started laying off my help," he explains. Although he had Blue Cross/ Blue Shield medical insurance, he says that his accountant made a mistake in submitting the names of employees who wanted to continue carrying their insurance. Duane's insurance was canceled instead of another employee's, and the mistake could not be corrected. His business was forced to declare bankruptcy. As if things weren't bad enough, his first wife died of breast cancer in 1993.

Things seemed to improve when Dee and Duane married in 1996. The couple moved nearer to the Nevada border from Tonopah, Arizona, at least partially because of Nevada wages, which were $34 an hour. That was nearly twice the wages in Arizona. Duane thought that by being just 20 miles from Nevada's border, he could join the Nevada union. But those wages never materialized. The September 11, 2001, terrorist attacks against the World Trade Center and the Pentagon took their toll on the construction business in his area: Many Nevada casinos canceled their plans to expand. Work already had slowed before September 11, but afterward there just wasn't enough construction work for the Southwest Carpenters Local.

As a result, both he and Dee lost their medical insurance. In addition, Duane was forced largely to live on $205 monthly in unemployment income. He already had been collecting unemployment for one year; it was due to expire shortly.

Even though the lucrative carpenter's job fell through in Nevada, all was not lost from the experience. The beauty of what is to be their new home serves as an even greater attraction.

The couple found their 2% breathtaking acres in Golden Valley, Arizona, after taking a day trip to Laughlin, Nevada, where they stayed in a casino. They stopped in a real estate office and were shown some vacant land.

They instantly liked the site. "They wanted $10,000," Duane says of the sellers. "We offered $8,000 with $1,600 down." The sellers carried the note.

The move to realize the couple's retirement dream hit yet another obstacle. They had put $3,000 into remodeling the mobile home they had bought for just $600 in Tonopah. They added a new kitchen, two bathrooms, and a bay window in the kitchen. Their plan was to bring it to Golden Valley to live in while they built their new home.

Unfortunately, specifications for mobile homes had changed over the years. Mohave County prohibited the Marks from moving the mobile home on to their new property. Today most mobile homes must be built with copper wiring rather than aluminum wiring. The Marks' mobile home still had the old-fashioned aluminum wiring.

Duane was able to sell the mobile home for $10,000, reaping more than a $6,000 profit. Plus, the buyers took a loan from him at a rate of 10 percent interest. "That helps out," he admits, noting that his loan generates an extra badly needed $320 in monthly income.

Upon their move to Golden Valley from Tonopah, Duane admits that he made some mistakes. He had started building in Tonopah, but it didn't work out, he explains. Nevertheless, he accumulated a lot of building materials and needed to rent trucks to haul it to Golden Valley. The rentals, materials, and motel bills were among the charges that went on credit cards. If he had it to do again, Duane says, he would have taken more time and made his move more slowly, relying more heavily on cash.

Duane has developed a very bad taste in his mouth for credit card issuers. "Most of the credit card companies I wouldn't deal with ever again in my life," he says. "They're just vultures. They play on people who have credit difficulties. They encourage their use."

Initially, he says, advertised rates were 18.9 percent or 21 percent. But before he knew it, rates had escalated to "more like 29 percent." On credit cards, higher rates often come if you make a late payment or exceed a credit line.

Today neither spouse routinely carries credit cards. Nor does either have a checking account. While checking accounts may be fine if you have a large balance, they believe, they can be trouble if you keep a $10 balance or rack up a lot of bounced check fees. They'd rather pay bills by money orders, which can be purchased for as little as 19 cents at convenience stores. Virtually all of Dee's Social Security now goes to paying off credit card debt. Duane expects, though, that by 2006, all the credit cards will be paid off. Their land should be paid off within the year, releasing more money to go toward the credit card debt and building materials.

Paying cash whenever they can helps. Duane says they always pay cash for cars. They recently bought their 1982 truck for $2,300. "We put $750 down and asked them to hold it for a couple of months, which they did. They fouled up my unemployment, so I had been going months without unemployment. I appealed it, and they sent us a check for $1,600. That's how we paid off the truck."

The Marks often rely on yard sales for materials. "We buy the materials we need for the house at garage sales and yard sales," Dee says. "We have to cut corners. We don't buy a whole lot of clothes. We don't spend a lot of money on ourselves. We just try to have a positive outlook."

This may not exactly sound like the Utopian retirement scenario just yet, we admit. But the two remain optimistic through all kinds of tough times.

Dee was fighting a problem with gall stones. In fact, she says she had "an attack" one month before our initial interview. She was turned away from a doctor due to a lack of health insurance. Even though a doctor two years earlier had told her she should have her gall bladder removed, she was trying to keep her condition under control with homeopathic remedies. She hoped that lecithin would help dissolve a gall stone. As we finally wrote this chapter, Dee was hospitalized and had her gall bladder removed. "We took her on Friday," Duane said five days afterward. "They refused to treat her. But someone told me if you go in an ambulance, they would take her. By Sunday, she was so bad, she was unable to sit up for more than a few minutes. So I called 911."

The Marks hope that the medical expense will be covered through the Arizona Health Care Cost Containment program (AHCCCS), Arizona's Medicaid program, and the State of Arizona's health care program for those who do not qualify for Medicaid. Their 1986 Ford Mustang also has been "down" because it needs a fuel pump.

Fortunately, at least a slight improvement already seems to be just around the corner. Duane planned to collect his Social Security in February 2003, when he turned 62. "I still plan to work," he says. One month after that, Dee, who already was collecting $424 monthly in Social Security, expected to be eligible for Medicare, solving her medical insurance problem. Duane was hoping that once he had a little more income, he, too, would be able to afford medical insurance.

The five-stage plans for the Marks' dream home are impressive. It will have a library, an atrium, a kitchen, a dinette, three bedrooms, and two baths.

As a carpenter, Duane was able to devise smart ways to save money on materials. At this writing—almost three years after starting his dream house—he had spent about $2,000 on materials.

However, he obtained most either for free or at very low cost. Often friends and neighbors in the area helped pitch in on the house or donated badly needed items.

Take the trailer they slept in: "That was like a God-send to us," Duane says. "We were sleeping in the storage shed." Some friends who had been building a straw bale house 50 miles from their site saved the day. They had a 1984 Aljo trailer that they had used while building their own house; the trailer was just sitting on their lot in disrepair. After the Marks had invited their friend to a cookout, he pulled Duane aside and offered the trailer for free. True, it needed repairs and the refrigerator didn't work. But there was nothing wrong with it that Duane couldn't easily fix. "It was a wonderful gift!" Duane says. "There are a lot of good people in the world."

The couple also obtained old appliances—much newer than the ones they previously had—from some people 10 miles from their home. Duane had done some work for them, and they were buying new appliances. "For part of the job, I got the old appliances. The refrigerator I bought from people moving from California. They sold it to us for $25. It was much nicer than the old one we brought up here."

Duane plans to use solar heat in his house. Solar panels will heat the water, which will be stored in a tank underground. The water then will be pumped through tubes in the floor. The solar panels were free in exchange for his labor removing them from a roof.

The outside of the house will be straw bales covered with stucco. Duane explains that the straw bales, often used in construction around Arizona, provide some of the best insulation at half the cost of traditional construction materials. The straw bales, which are stacked like bricks, also are environmentally friendly because they use recycled straw. Although many in his area build homes of straw bales exclusively, he is combining the straw bales with wood-frame walls, which he anticipates will be much sturdier.

Duane was able to get wood pallets for his walls for free. Pallets, he explains, are routinely used for shipping. Companies that deliver beer, for example, will set it on pallets. "If you drive around an industrial area, you see stacks of them outside of factories and trucking companies. You can ask them if they'd like to get rid of them." Some companies will pick up the pallets and dispose of them, so you actually could buy a whole truck-load of pallets for $25. "But I did it the hard way before I discovered that I could do that." The result: He obtained his wood for free. He expects that the house will take about 2,000 pallets.

Duane didn't need the expensive services of an architect, either. "I've drawn plans for various companies all my life," he explains.

If Duane had built his dream home all at once, it would have required some $1,400 worth of building permits, he figures. That was unaffordable. Instead, he is doing it in five phases. So far, he has been required to get three permits, costing at least $300. Meanwhile, he buys recycled stock steel studs and lumber whenever he can. "There's a place in Phoenix where I can get used lumber." Not only are steel studs cheap, he says, but they help save trees.

Now, used lumber is a very touchy issue. 'The county frowned on it. But I know what good lumber is because I've worked with it all my life. I can cut off the good parts." More than four decades of carpentry experience has taught him that cheaper used lumber often can be better than new lumber. In fact, because it's seasoned, it's less likely to warp. If you want lumber today that won't warp, he says, you need to pay dearly for it.

He admits that on one inspection, the building inspector was skeptical about the idea of using used lumber. But once he saw that Duane clearly was cutting away the bad parts of the wood and knew what he was doing, the permit was approved.

Anybody can build a house, regardless of skills, Duane firmly believes. Of course, he says, it's more difficult to do on a slim budget. But there are books available that guide you through every step. "There are women out here who haven't ever picked up a hammer who have built a house," Duane says. Some of the more difficult tasks are pouring cement slabs and putting in a septic tank, if there is no city sewage system, he says. "But with a little bit of ingenuity and thought, it can be done. Trading labor is one way. There are always people who would be willing to help if you help them."

The same friend who had donated a trailer also helped them get carpeting for it. The deal was arranged with an area hotel that was discarding it. "We bought mini-blinds at Home Depot and cut them to fit the windows," Duane says. "My wife made some valances to go over the top of the blinds. The valances hang on some welded-together horseshoes, which act as brackets. We're going to loop a lariat rope over the horseshoes."

The Marks say they would not ask their children for money. After all, they have their own obligations. Fortunately, they have met great friends in their neighborhood who help out occasionally. For example, if they travel, it typically costs $5 per day per animal to have someone care for them. Already that's a price tag of $25 per day for five animals. For their upcoming holiday trip, two sets of neighbors volunteered to watch the animals for two weeks apiece.

"That's been a big factor for us," Duane says. "Our neighbors are very helpful. It's a close-knit community and we work together. When we first bought property, one neighbor was having a yard sale or a drive sale. We stopped in and talked to them and got to know them a little bit."

Before finally moving to Golden Valley, the couple took short trips to the area for about seven months to install a fence and build their storage area. "People would stop in and say, 'We live over here and over there.'" They often asked if they could be of any help. The Marks' closest neighbor, from California, often helped out with projects.

The couple spent Thanksgiving with some 16 neighbors at a friend's house. Right now the Marks lack room for such affairs, although Dee has invited friends to their shed for breakfast or lunch. Soon, she says, that will change. A 2,800-square-foot home will sit on their lot, dotted with grease wood bushes, a few cacti, and yucca plants.

The Marks already have a kitchen and sitting room in a storage shed on their property. Also standing is the foundation framing for a bathroom. Their three cats are lodged in a screened-in porch with an awning. "We had two little sheds out in the back to store some stuff," Duane says. "Rats got into that, so we enclosed and screened in the porch, and use that for storage. That's going to be our next room." Two dogs, including a 250-pound Great Dane, are kept in a 60-square-foot yard surrounded by a 6-foot chain-link fence.

Admits Dee, "It's been a rough road. We've both been through so much. We've learned by experience in our lives. We've had the good and the bad. Now we're trying to get ahead. We've been there and done that. We're older and wiser and know that material things aren't everything. We can communicate. We talk about our feelings."

When they get down, their dream house keeps them going. "It's going to be a beautiful home when it's done," Dee says. "We shared our ideas. We talked about different colors together. We want an atrium. We're going to have an atrium. We both picked out plants, and we're going to have a pond. We looked at the fish we want to put in the pond. We have a lot of pictures of things and color schemes we both like. We've got it all in files.

"(Duane) likes to write. In the home we're going to have a library where we can do writing. I like hobbies and crafts. We've made some crafts, and we went to craft shows a couple of years ago."

Their lives definitely were not as bad as they once were. And they anticipate that in just a few years, their lives should be much, much better. They will be able to use income from their Social Security to enjoy life, and perhaps, travel rather than to buy materials for their dream home and pay off debt.

"In three years, we'll have everything paid off, a clear mortgage, no house payment, and no land payment," Dee says. 'Then we can start new goals."

"We'd like to take the trailer on road trips," Duane muses. "I'd like to take Dee to Idaho, where I lived. I have some relatives in Washington I'd like to visit."

Doing It Yourself

What can you do if, like the Marks, you have health problems and you're having tough times financially? There is some good news. Most people are entitled to certain federal benefits when they retire.

Social Security

Everybody who works and pays Social Security taxes or FICA taxes may be entitled to collect Social Security benefits, provided that they've worked long enough. If you were born in 1929 or later, you need to have worked 10 years to qualify. Those born before that date may need fewer years to qualify.

When you can start to collect Social Security ratchets upward depending upon your year of birth For those born through 1937, the full retirement age is 65. For each birth year after that, the full retirement age increases in two-month increments until it settles at 66 for those born between 1943 and 1954. And for those born after 1954, the full retirement age increases in two-month increments until it settles at 67 for those born in 1960 or later. To determine your exact full retirement age, you can go to www.ssa.gov/retirechartred.htm.

Regardless of your date of birth, you can start to collect benefits at age 62, but you'll earn less than you would if you wait until you hit the full retirement age. On the other hand, if you delay your retirement beyond the full retirement age, you stand to collect more.

Social Security calculates your earnings based on the 35 years in which you earned the most. If you'd like to see how much you're entitled to based on current earnings, visit www. socialsecurity.gov. You also may be eligible for cost-of-living benefit increases starting with the year you become 62.

A spouse is entitled to half of the retired worker's full benefit unless he or she collects before reaching full retirement age. If you have disabled or minor children eligible for Social Security, each can earn up to half of your full benefit.

Widows or widowers also can obtain benefits starting at age 60 (50 if disabled). They may switch to their own benefits as early as age 62. Divorced spouses may be entitled to benefits based on their ex-spouse's Social Security record.

Once you hit the month that's considered your full retirement age, you still can work and receive Social Security benefits. However, if you take your benefits any earlier, you could suffer a reduction in earnings if you earn more than the specified limits.

Medicare

Another nice benefit that you're entitled to once you reach age 65 is Medicare. Medicare Part A covers hospitals, skilled nursing facilities, hospice care, and limited home health care. Medicare Part B covers other treatments, including doctor visits, outpatient care, and physical and occupational therapy.

Unfortunately, you are required to pay for Part B. A premium—$58.70 in 2003—is deducted monthly from your Social Security check.

Beware: Medicare does not cover 100 percent of your healthcare costs. For example, it may not cover your deductible. Nor may it cover prescriptions or care outside the United States. You'll need to purchase private health insurance to cover what Medicare does not. These policies, known as "Medigap," must follow state and federal laws. A woman age 80, for example, would pay about $160 monthly for Medigap coverage. In evaluating MediGap policies, it is important to compare services offered. Also, look for restrictions on pre-existing conditions and the terms under which premiums may increase. But the total cost still should be much cheaper than a private individual health insurance policy.

For more information about Medicare, call 1-800-633-4247 or go online at www.medicare.gov.

Medicaid

Can't afford Medicare gap coverage? Or are you too young to qualify for Medicare? Medicaid, a joint federal-state program administered by the states, provides medical assistance for individuals and families with low incomes. It may pay for doctors and hospital stays as well as long-term nursing home coverage, home health care, medical supplies, and equipment.

Here are the requirements to qualify for Medicaid, which could be offered under a state program of a different name.

Individuals are typically required to have no more than the following:
- $2,000 in assets
- A burial fund of $1,500
- A home, a car, and jewelry

A couple typically can have no more than the following:

- $3,000 in assets
- Two $1,500 burial funds
- Assets such as a car, jewelry, and clothes
- A home

A number of states have income caps to qualify for Medicaid. If you live in any of the following states, you can't get Medicaid if your income exceeds a particular threshold: Alabama, Arkansas, Florida, Louisiana, New Mexico, South Carolina, Wyoming, Alaska, Colorado, Idaho, Mississippi, South Dakota, Arizona, Delaware, Iowa, Nevada, Oregon, and Texas.

Regardless of whether you live in state with an income eligibility cap, there often is a look-back period, typically 36 months. This means that for three years before your application for Medicaid, you must meet the income and asset eligibility requirements.

All gross income is counted, including Social Security, Veterans Administration benefits, pensions, and income from mortgages.

Medicaid typically covers people who are receiving other types of federal aid. For more information, visit www.cms.hhs.gov.

Other Health-Care Solutions

New York elder law attorney Peter J. Strauss suggests that if you're leaving a job and your company has more than 20 employees, you might be able to continue under your employer's group plan for 18 months. Of course, you'll have to pay your own way. If you're disabled, he says, you can stay on the plan for 29 months.

He also advises that even if you have a health problem, you should check with your state to see if you're able to get health insurance. In certain states, including New York, you can buy insurance without medical underwriting—regardless of whether you already have a medical problem.

Also, individual states may have programs that pay some or all of Medicare premiums. Plus, they may pay Medicare deduc-tibles and coinsurance for certain people who have Medicare and have a low income.

For emergencies, you can always go to the emergency room. Federal law requires hospitals to treat and stabilize anyone in an emergency—regardless of their ability to pay. However, notes Ron Pollack, executive director of Families USA in Washington, D.C., "this only applies to people who are at immediate risk of life or limb. Even if you have a serious illness, it does not apply."

The hospital and doctors likely will bill you for services. If you can't pay, you may be able to work out a payment plan. "There is no guarantee that the provider will be willing to do that," Pollack warns. "There is no law today that guarantees someone will get health care if they're uninsured. You may be able to get charitable care, care from a public hospital or teaching hospital, or care from a community health center. But none of these things provides any guarantee that you're going to get the care that you need. Most people who are uninsured delay getting care because they feel they can't afford to pay for it. In some cases, it might work out fine, and in other instances, it does not and can lead to tragic consequences." As a last resort, you may have to declare bankruptcy. But that's a small price to pay to be saved from a life-threatening illness.

Some other places to look are your state's low-income healthcare coverage or your union's health-care coverage. If you are a veteran or military retiree, you may be able to get health-care benefits. Veterans can call the U.S. Department of Veteran Affairs at 1-800-827-1000. If you or your spouse is retired from the military, call the Department of Defense at 1-800-538-9552 for more information.

Other Sources of Financial Aid

Supplemental Security Income (SSI) is a cash assistance program administered by the Social Security Administration. It provides financial assistance to the aged, blind, or disabled individuals with little or no income.

To be eligible for SSI in 2003, you must meet the following criteria:

- Be age 65 or older, blind, or disabled
- Be a U.S. citizen, but certain legal immigrants may be eligible
- Have countable resources that total no more than $2,000
- Have income less than $552 a month for individuals in their own households

Even though you probably hate to do it, you might look into your state's food stamp program if you have no other choice. The program is designed so that low-income families can buy nutritious food with coupons and electronic benefits transfer (EBT) cards.

Generally, to qualify, households in 2003 could have no more than $2,000 in "countable resources," such as a bank account, and $3,000 if one person is at least 60 years old or disabled. A household of one could have a gross income no higher than $960 and a net income no higher than $739. For a household of two, those income figures increased to a $1,294 gross or $995 net. However, there may be exceptions.

To find out about more about the food stamp program in your state, visit www.fns.usda.gov.

Chapter 5

Edgar and Betty Plunkett: Retiring Early in Belize

What can you do when you're too young to get your company's retirement benefits or Social Security? Edgar Plunkett, a former lineman/serviceman for the electric company, and his wife, Betty, solved this problem together after a great deal of research. They bought a waterfront home in Belize—a Central American country the size of Massachusetts—and retired in 1999 on a stash of some $500,000.

Although Betty, 59, often misses the flounder they were able to catch off the coast of Nordi Carolina, they now enjoy fishing for barracuda, snook, or jack crevalles in their kayak. Tarpon can weigh in the 100-pound range. "I haven't gotten one in yet," says Ed, 61, ruefully. "But I've hooked some."

The Plunketts are busy almost every day of the week with card games, dinners, and other activities in their Consejo Shores development. "It's been our experience that retirement can be fattening," Betty says. "We basically live in a retirement community where everyone is just one big family. We do everything together. Many of us meet regularly at our favorite nearby restaurant, Smuggler's Den, Friday night for burger and fries or pizza, and Sundays for traditional rice and beans or roast beef. It's common for everyone to meet after dinner at someone's home for desserts, coffee, and card games."

A half-million dollars might sound like a lot. But at today's interest rates, it would not have gone very far had the couple remained in their beachfront condo in Carolina Beach, North Carolina.

"We couldn't have stayed in the home we were in," Betty says. "We might have been able to retire in the States if we had moved to a trailer park." Their lifestyle would have suffered drastically, she believes. The couple estimates that at this writing, they can live in Belize for $1,000 monthly. Had they remained in the States, they expect it would cost at least twice that—even though their condo on the beach was mortgage-free.

Both spouses had previously been married. Betty came into the marriage with two children, and Ed had four. They already had experienced a taste of living in a foreign country when Ed worked for ARAMCO in Saudi Arabia. The two had lived on one paycheck—the smaller one—and banked the larger check through direct deposit to the United States. With their savings, they were able to pay cash for their condo in North Carolina when they returned.

Initially, there were some bad experiences with their investments. They had a large amount of their money in no-load mutual funds. When the stock market crashed in December 1987, they panicked. Instead of riding it out, they cashed out of stock funds and switched to an insurance company—a move they now admit was a mistake.

Immediately after that "Black Monday" crash, the stock market rebounded and continued to skyrocket for several years afterward. Meanwhile, the insurance company they invested in began having problems and subsequently was acquired by another. Although the couple got their money back, it meant time and lost income from their investment.

The Plunketts had been dissatisfied with their broker but subsequently lined up with another, with whom they are very pleased. The Wachovia Securities broker helped prepare them for early retirement. At the broker's suggestion, they diversified their investments more. The broker put some money that wasn't in their IRA into growth stock funds, with the aim of producing a greater return.

"Eventually, when we decided to make our move, we could switch into some income-producing funds," Ed says. By putting the money outside their IRA into growth funds, the broker reasoned, they still would have their IRAs to tap when the time came.

Ed was beginning to feel the aches and pains of his grueling job, which involved climbing poles and digging ditches. The couple had just returned to the United States from Saudi Arabia, where Ed had a desk job. His newer U.S. job sometimes meant he worked as many as 30 hours straight in a very fast-growing area prone to hurricanes. He was finding it hard to handle.

Betty knew that things could only get worse for him as he aged. She did not want him working such a difficult job until he was 62 or 65, the standard retirement age. She already had stopped working, turning down temporary odd jobs she previously had accepted. Fortunately, Betty saw the writing on the wall and began using her computer to surf the Internet in search of lower-cost places to retire.

Ed says that the couple had hoped he could retire at 55. But they started calculating the expenses. "You've got federal tax, which we had to pay," he says. "There was state tax, city tax, and county tax. Plus, we lived in a condominium, so there was association maintenance and flood insurance."

The expenses reached a crescendo when property taxes started on an upward spiral. When the couple left, Ed estimates that they ran some $2,000 annually. He figured they would only continue to rise. "The price (assessed value) of property was practically double almost every year," he says.

By contrast, in Belize, they pay a land tax of close to $150 in U.S. dollars each year. Overall, the couple estimates that they save more than $1,500 a month living in Latin America.

Ed says that with his job, he would not have been eligible for retirement benefits until he turned 65. He figured that even if he waited it out, it would mean a difference of only a few hundred dollars more per month. "I said it just wasn't worth it. We started looking for places that were a little bit more reasonable to live."

The couple finally put their North Carolina condo on the market. Although it took close to one year to sell, they were able to load up just enough of their belongings to fit into a pickup truck. They moved to Belize in 1999. They say $182,000 of their retirement stash came from the sale of their home.

Betty says that the chief force that influenced the couple to choose Belize was the book *Belize Retirement Guide* (Preview Pub 1999), by Bill and Claire Grey. A flyer about the book had arrived at their home after she had signed on to a website seeking information about retirement options abroad. It was enticing, boasting that you could retire in that country for $350 monthly. The most recent edition of the book, however, has since raised that cost of living to $450 monthly.

Betty issues a stern warning: Depending upon your lifestyle, the country may not be cheap at all. In fact, published reports have indicated that Belize actually is more expensive than the United States. At this writing, though, Betty estimates that if you're careful, you can live in Belize at a cost of about $450 per person—or $900 per couple.

Ed had been particularly attracted to the fact that English, rather than Spanish, is the primary language in Belize. Belize was a former British colony.

The couple also began favoring Belize when they learned that there were difficulties buying property on the waterfront in Mexico. Many who had thought they owned property actually owned a 100-year lease, she says. There are no such rules in Belize, and the couple definitely wanted to live on the water, much like they had in North Carolina. Mexico seemed to have more red tape for retirees seeking to immigrate, they add.

"We decided to go check it out for ourselves," Betty says. The couple took a flight to Cancun and a five-hour bus ride from Cancun to Belize. "We carried the book along with us," she says. "We actually met other people on the same trip, carrying the same book."

On the couple's first trip to Belize, they fell in love with the area. They made some friends at a guesthouse where they stayed. The owner of the hotel and her daughter helped to provide information about the area.

The Plunketts decided in advance, from research on the Internet, that the area they liked was Corozal. The chief reason was its proximity to Mexico. Corozal is in the northern part of the country, which also is drier. "The farther south you go, the wetter it is," Betty says. The area also is less prone to sand fleas.

The couple discovered, however, that the book that promised a cost of living of $350 immediately was outdated. "I would recommend that anybody check it out by yourself." The first two-week trip was aimed at examining the cost of living, the climate, and the area itself.

"On the second trip, we started looking for a place to live. We had intended to rent a year or two before we started looking, but we couldn't wait." They had been renting a small wooden house on the water for $250 monthly, which was not cheap by Belize standards at the time. They found their home, about 7 miles outside Corozal Town, in just six months and went ahead and bought it.

The couple had been driving around the area when they spotted the home and bought it from the son of the developer of their Consejo Shores development. In 1999, they paid $84,000. The couple feared, however, that their house could be a problem if left in their estate. "To us, this would not be considered a good investment property unless you wanted it as a long-term investment. Ed's grown son agreed to pay for half of the home. In exchange, the home will be his when they're gone. "That's one reason we were able to buy a nicer home," Betty adds. "It was a blessing for us and a good investment for our son as he loves Belize and the home that will one day be his."

The home they bought was a modest 1,000 square feet made of concrete. It has no closets and no garage. "Belizeans do not put closets in their homes," Betty notes. "There is no such thing as closets." Although she still misses having a garage, Ed since has built a closet for their bedroom and bought a wardrobe for their second bedroom. Plus, they have added a screened-in room and small porch in front, extending their home another 500 square feet. On it sits a hammock.

Apart from some three years of research on the retirement location, the couple had little in the way of a retirement plan. "We just wanted to retire at age 55," Betty says. "We didn't quite make it. But we always saved. It was a lifestyle with us. We always lived below our means. It just made sense to us. We clipped coupons, went to discount movie theaters, and bargain-shopped. Just generally we were careful with our money and never thought of living any other way. We didn't consider it a burden at all—rather, a challenge." The couple never believed in paying interest. They pay off credit card bills monthly.

Today the Plunketts can see Chetumal, Mexico, from their 1,500-square-foot home overlooking a bay. The Mexican town is just a 10-minute boat ride away in their kayak or a 20-minute drive.

They generally have access to a swimming pool, which is part of a hotel. But at this writing, Betty says, the hotel was up for sale and the pool was closed. Since retiring, the two have been able to hire a maid to clean their home weekly at a cost of just about $12 in U.S. currency.

Betty never had a maid when she worked. "Isn't it odd that I had to retire to experience that?" she says. The price is similar for yard work. Although those prices might seem low, "it's a very fair salary for Belizians," she says. "I don't think they're exploited." The couple, which has about half of an acre of land, do some of the work themselves. And while it rarely costs more than $10 for the two to eat out in a restaurant, there are more expensive restaurants available.

Butane for cooking and hot water costs $25 U.S. dollars monthly; piped water runs $7.50 monthly and trash removal costs $10 monthly. Betty stresses, though, that Belize is not necessarily as cheap as some might expect. For example, electricity in Belize is considered about the most expensive in its region. An Internet brochure touting their development indicated that electricity typically costs $75 to $125 U.S. dollars monthly for normal use. Even though the Plunketts have an air-conditioner, they do not use it. They speculate that others who use their air-conditioner may not have a cost of living as low as theirs. Their highest electric bill since they had been there, as of January 2003, was $75.

Telephone calls to the United Sates range from $1 to $1.60 per minute, and Internet service averages $2 per hour, with a minimum of 20 hours monthly. Very few online shopping sites accept a foreign address, she says, so many Americans maintain mailboxes at places such as The UPS Store.

Ed does most of the work on the home. "He loves doing it," she says. Also, it's not easy to find skilled workers. "If you want it done right, you're better off doing it yourself." The couple uses Betty's sister's address in the United States for anything they need. "It's best to keep a U.S. address—even if it's just a relative or a friend's," she advises.

"If you go somewhere to buy something—and I'm not talking about the grocery store—there definitely is what you would call a 'gringo' price." In fact, Betty says, there even are special prices for Belizeans who dress as though they might have money. "That goes on everywhere in third-world countries."

If you walk into a store and can't find what you want, chances are, they'll offer to order it for you, Betty says. Don't expect it to arrive in one or two weeks, though. "That might mean six months. It's a bit frustrating. You have to learn to just relax."

The couple did buy a small four-door pick-up truck in Belize, even though it is expensive to own a car or truck. "The duty is really very, very high on vehicles," she warns. "It depends on the type of vehicle." Their four-door, four-cylinder pickup truck requires less duty. "Of course, the four-door model is the most convenient, and everyone needs to haul something in Belize. Diesel is more economical to run." Plus, it is one of the most appropriate vehicles for Belize's rugged roads.

Of the lifestyle in Belize, Betty warns, "It's really different. 'You don't use all modern appliances. I don't know a single person here who has a dishwasher. That's something I thought I couldn't live without at one time. It doesn't bother me in the least."

The Plunketts drink bottled water. Although most homes have a large drainwater system, their house does not. Ultimately, they hope to build one that will filter water so they can drink it. Water is extremely hard, according to Betty.

The couple advises that you bring your own electronics to Belize if you move there, but keep in mind that they are likely to deteriorate in the hot and humid climate without air-conditioning.

"The very best may be a waste of good money," she says. "The best DVD player might be preferable to a VCR because tapes deteriorate very quickly. Overstuffed upholstered furniture doesn't fare well in such a climate." Also think about purchasing furniture locally rather than importing it, Betty recommends. "Custom made solid wood furniture is reasonable." You also can buy major appliances at reasonable prices— unless you want American brands, she says.

Property and casualty insurance aren't quite the same as in the United States. The Plunketts have car insurance, purchased thorough a Belizean friend. The premiums are a lot lower than in the United States, but the insurance doesn't cover as much.

Although they could purchase homeowners insurance in Belize, they don't bother with it. "It's a little iffy as to whether you can collect on it," she says. "They have lots of little rules— especially living on the water. Of course, we have a concrete house. They will not insure anything other than a concrete house. We had insurance for a while, and then we talked to other people. Most of us decided not to carry it. They don't cover theft unless you have burglar bar protection on every window. It's like Ed told the insurance agent, 'If I have burglar bar protection, I don't need your insurance.'" The couple carry liability insurance only on their truck. Their life insurance consists of a $10,000 policy that Ed got on his job.

One of the couple's chief concerns is health care. They have no health insurance. However, they say, some clinics in Belize will treat people who can't afford it for free. Plus, they are very close to Merida, Mexico, where they figure they would go if they need surgery. Prices there are about a quarter of what they cost in the United States.

"Our closest friends are doing the same thing we are," she says. "They've dropped all medical insurance. It's not affordable on this kind of income." She says she knows some people who have had to move back to the States due to medical problems.

The Belize Social Security system is no panacea. The Plunketts do keep a Belize Social Security card. However, Belize Social Security benefits are available only to the self-employed, employees, nationals, legal residents, refugees, and those with work permits who have contributed to the system.

Nevertheless, it's worth carrying the card. Retirees with legal residential status who have never worked or contributed to social security may be entitled to discounts or benefits offered by some 186 businesses or organizations under the program. Some of the benefits listed by businesses include access to a restroom. Betty notes that often there is a charge to use public restroom facilities.

Crime also is a problem. The Plunketts say that most homes, including theirs, have burglar bars on their windows, and they've already had two bicycles stolen. "It's a third-world country," Betty says. "The general consensus is, you have to watch out for yourself. You are a foreigner. They consider us to be very wealthy. You are definitely a target for crime."

Police forces in Belize are small and underfunded. She estimates that the police force for the district of Corozal, which spans several villages, including Corozal, consists of just two vehicles. "So, you can't always depend on them to be able to be where you would like them to be if you need them." When there have been crimes, the police do make a conscientious effort to come out, she says. "They patrol. There have been some arrests at times, and they even have recovered some stolen goods. You have to give them credit for what they do, considering the resources they have."

Despite the drawbacks, Betty says they have had no problems at all from day one, largely because they have done so much research that they knew what to expect.

The couple keeps financial accounts in the United States— except for the minimum amount in U.S. dollars to hold their retiree status in Belize.

Upon moving to Belize, the Plunketts took advantage of the Belize Retirement Program, which is aimed at attracting foreigners and their capital to the country. The benefits of the program include the ability to import personal effects and an approved means of transportation free of import duties and taxes. It also exempts income from sources outside of Belize from taxes.

It does not, however, necessarily exempt income from U.S. taxes.

The Plunketts have a bank account at the Bank of Nova Scotia, which, they say, is backed by the Canadian government but still qualifies for the account requirement under the Belize retirement plan. At this writing, the requirement to qualify as a "Qualified Retired Person" was $2,000 in monthly income from a pension or annuity generated outside Belize. The Belize Tourism Board says a person also must be at least 45 years old and pay certain fees. For more information, see www.belizeretirement.org.

The couple admits that with the bear market that has lasted close to three years at this writing, their assets have declined quite a bit, but not enough to have much effect on their lifestyle.

So far, they merely are tightening their belts. "We need a new television, but we're putting it off," Betty says. "We can use a new lawnmower but will keep repairing this one. I need a new range. I'm still using the range that was in the house when we moved in, but it's not in very good shape."

Ed says that their broker has been very good about keeping in touch with them during this trying time. "Anytime he has a question about anything, he gives us a call down here. We send him an e-mail and he calls us right back—sometimes in a couple of hours."

Recently, the couple says, they moved more of their money into lower-risk bonds. Although the economy may be hurting assets in the

United States, Betty says the economy seems to be improving in their area of Belize. That, she says, is because the area around where they are has been designated as a duty-free zone. Mexicans can come to Belize and shop without paying duty, and a great deal of construction is underway.

Right now, she says, the couple is just hoping that the U.S. economy will improve and that their income will increase. They largely have given up travel. Nevertheless, she says, "We are looking forward to next year when Ed applies for (U.S.) Social Security. We were hoping then that we could start doing a little traveling."

Doing It Yourself

The Plunketts were smart to begin preparing ahead of time for their early retirement. As you get ready to retire, experts usually advise that you begin shifting to low-risk investments that are sure to pay you monthly income. Here are some low-risk options to consider:

- Treasury securities
- Bank deposits (certificates of deposit and money market accounts)
- Money market mutual funds
- Short-term government bonds and bond funds
- Insured municipal bonds is Fixed annuities

Treasury securities are an ultra-safe place to put your hard-earned cash and are backed by Uncle Sam. Unfortunately, at this writing, yields are at a 40-year low. U.S. Treasury securities that mature in up to two years are paying less than 2 percent.

Good old-fashioned bank deposits, such as certificates of deposits and money market accounts, may be one of your safest bets, and it's possible to find banks that will let you invest as little as $100. Your principal and interest on deposits are guaranteed to $100,000 per person by the U.S. government-backed Federal Deposit Insurance Corporation (FDIC).

Certificates of deposit (CDs) typically pay a little more than a money market deposit account and mature in terms ranging from three months to five years or more. At the time of this writing, it was tough to get much mileage from the interest on CDs. On average, one-year CDs yielded just 2 percent, and five-year CDs yielded 3.54 percent.

With a money market deposit account (MMDA), however, you have the convenience of writing a maximum of three checks monthly to persons other than yourself.

Consider joining a credit union. Credit unions typically pay half of a percent more on their deposit accounts and CDs. Call 1-800-358-5710 or visit www.cuna.org to track down a credit union that you might be eligible to join. As long as they are backed by the National Credit Union Administration, federally insured credit unions have the same U.S. government guarantee as the FDIC.

Another option for finding better interest rates is to look online at www.bankrate.com. You can earn up to 1 percent more by shopping nationwide.

Historically, money market mutual funds, which invest in U.S. government securities and carry the guarantee of the investment company that you won't lose principal, have paid more than bank money market deposit accounts, no more. At this writing, they paid slightly over .50 percent.

Short-term government bonds and bond funds invest in U.S. government securities that mature in less than two years. They pay slightly higher yields than money market funds, but they do not guarantee your principal if you sell them.

When you invest in a short-term U.S. government bond, you don't have to worry about the investment defaulting. However, if interest rates rise, your short-term bond could decline in value if you go to sell it.

Professionally managed short-term bond mutual funds invest in a large number of bonds that mature in two years or less. The fund managers shorten the maturity of the bonds when rates are rising.

Some no-load short-term bond funds to consider, according to Morningstar, Inc., in Chicago, include these:

- Dreyfus Short-Intermediate Term Government Fund (DSIGX)—Contact Dreyfus for more information at 1-800-373-9387.
- Vanguard Short-Term Federal (VSGBX)—Contact Vanguard for more information at 1-800-662-7447.
- American Century Short-Term Government Fund (TWUSX)—Contact American Century at 1-800-638-5660.

Another way to earn low-risk attractive yields is in insured municipal bonds. But beware: These are not backed by the U.S. government. That's why they pay a little more. At this writing, they yielded around 3.5 percent tax-free. Even if you are in the 27 percent tax bracket, that translates into a taxable equivalent yield of 4.8 percent. Someone in a higher tax bracket could earn a taxable equivalent yield of 5.1 percent.

When you invest in a municipal bond, you collect semi-annual interest. At maturity, you get your principal back. It is easy to sell your insured municipal bond before it matures. However, bond prices and interest rates move in opposite directions. So, if interest rates rise, the value of the bond will decline if you sell it.

Municipal bonds are sold in units of $5,000. If you have more than $5,000, you can buy bonds that mature in different years. So you can reinvest the maturing bonds at higher rates. That way, you can roll over the money into new bonds that pay higher rates.

"Insured municipal bonds are safe," says Dian Vujovich, publisher of Allaboutfunds.com. "The yields are great for people in any tax bracket. But you have to buy and hold the bonds to maturity so you get your principal back."

If you have less than $5,000, consider insured municipal bond funds. However, be careful. Bond funds do not mature because the fund manager constantly is buying and selling bonds. Therefore, with a bond fund, you are not guaranteed to get your principal back.

Two of the highest-rated insured bond funds by Morningstar, Inc., in Chicago, include:

- Vanguard Insured Long-Term Tax-Exempt Fund (VILPX)— Contact Vanguard for more information at 1-800-662-7447.
- Franklin Insured Tax-Free Income A (FFLTX)—Contact Franklin for more information at 1-800-342-5236. (This fund carries a 4.25 percent front-end load or commission.)

Fixed annuities are contracts with insurance companies. They pay a rate set by the insurance company that issues them. With a fixed annuity, your money grows tax-deferred until your contract requires you to cash out the annuity or begin receiving income for life. Depending on how the insurance company structures the annuity, you can hold on to it until you are 75 years old or older. At that time, you can cash out the annuity and pay income tax on your earnings. Or, you can convert it to an "immediate annuity" and receive periodic checks for life. At the time of this writing, you can get an annuity yielding 5 percent.

Understanding Property and Joint Ownership

Particularly if you are retiring to another country, like the Plunketts did, it is important to keep good records of properties, warns David Connell, a Mexican corporate foreign investment lawyer in Ixtapa, Guerrero.

Connell says that deeds need to be referenced to or attached to wills. "I have quite a few clients saying their parents own property in Mexico somewhere, but they don't know where it is. If we have absolutely no information, it's very difficult to locate the property."

Meanwhile, the Plunketts had good reason to jointly own property with Ed's son. But Connell says that ordinarily, unless there are some foreign tax issues, people should think long and hard about having property joindy owned with a son or daughter.

For one thing, if a property is jointly owned with a minor, there could be special problems. In Mexico, if your child is under the age of 18 and there is property in his or her name, the only way property can be sold is through a court order. "Don't think you're going to represent your child and sell the property," he says.

Lee R. Phillips, co-author of *Protecting Your Financial Future* (Legalees 1999), has long been outspoken against joint ownership—even in the United States. If you put a child's name on the deed of your home and you ultimately want to sell it, you could have a problem if the child doesn't want to sell it, Phillips says. Children can go bad, go bankrupt, or go through an ugly divorce, he warns.

Assuming that the value you are granting your son or daughter is greater than $11,000, you could be forced to pay U.S. gift tax if you give the child part ownership. You also risk creating further problems for your child if you become incapacitated.

Once you make the child a joint owner, he adds, you're in even more trouble if you change your mind and take the child's name off the deed. In that case, Uncle Sam gets to collect gift tax again. And the joint owner could be saddled with income tax as well.

Phillips notes that most people become incompetent 90 days before they die. If the property is owned joindy, it may not be able to be sold without the signature of the joint owner. If one person needs to sell and the other owner can't sign, the joint owner might have to get a court to appoint a conservator or guardian for the other joint owner.

Chapter 6

Alan and Sandra Clark: King and Queen of the Road

After considering early retirement for five years, Alan, 62, and Sandra "Sandy" Clark, 57, finally took the plunge in June 2000. They sold their house and all their possessions and began traveling full-time with a truck and a one-bedroom recreational vehicle. Both had no retirement benefits through their employers, so there was no major reason for them to postpone their retirement any longer. "We didn't feel like we were going to get ahead," Sandy says. "We were just going to stay in the same place and tread water."

When we caught up with the couple, they were helping Sandy's sister get settled into her new home in California. Their daily attire is a T-shirt and jeans. In the two and a half years they have been on the road, they've traveled leisurely through Wyoming, Idaho, Montana, the western part of Canada (Alberta and British Columbia), Washington, Oregon, the California coastline, Colorado, Kansas, and Arkansas.

Alan and Sandy say they had been hearing too many stories of people getting to retirement age and not being well enough to do what they wished. "We felt we were young enough and had our health," Sandy says. "We wanted to do it now. As a friend of mine used to say, 'If you sit around and wait for all the lights to turn green, you're never going to make it out of town.'"

Their hypothesis was right. Sandy says that since the two retired, she has suffered less from the back problems that plagued her when she was working. "We're not tired all the time," she adds.

"We've had a lot more pleasure and a lot less stress," Alan agrees. "Better overall health. People need to understand that they don't need all the material things in life."

The couple was quite ready to leave their home in Colorado Springs. Their children were grown and their house was larger than they needed. In addition, the city was getting larger than they liked. They evaluated their options. Neither spouse had ever been inclined to travel abroad, "for no real reason other than the fact that there's just so much to see in every little town in America," Alan says. "So I think the attraction was just to get out and see what else is in the country—get off the beaten path and get off the interstate highways."

In their working lives, the couple had managed to save $450,000—including $235,000 from the sale of their home. At the time the couple began their odyssey, the bear market had not heavily ravaged the country and their financial situation looked attractive. "We had both contributed to our IRAs (individual retirement accounts). I had a SEP (simplified employee pension) account," Alan says. "We had a nice annuity that we set up a few years before."

Before making their move, Alan had worked as a commercial real estate broker. He wound down his job and informed his clients months ahead of his intentions to retire. He began transferring his jobs to other brokers within his group before he gave 30 days notice. When we interviewed him, he was continuing to receive some leftover income from that job, but was expecting his social security to replenish that income when it stops. Sandy, who had been doing administrative work for a defense contractor, gave a one-month notice before giving up her $40,000-plus annual salary. Sandy began realizing that defense contracts would come and go for her company, and with the growing lack of defense business before September 11, 2001, she could soon find herself laid off. That never happened. However, it started the wheels turning in their minds.

During their working life, the couple originally truly enjoyed their Coleman pop-up tent trailer together. "We tend not to have a lot in common—unfortunately," Sandy chuckles, "but we've both always loved camping." The couple saw some information in a magazine about a Life on Wheels school, and in 1995, the two sent in their reservations to attend the series of classes in Moscow, Idaho.

"It's a one-week program," Alan says. "They provide places for your RV if you have one. The first two times we went, we had our tent trailer. The third time we went was just about three weeks after we started full-timing. We wanted to go back and say, 'Now here we are, so now what do we do?'" Initially, they were among seven couples in the class and they learned quite a bit. By their third session, attendance had swelled to some 700 couples.

Classes focused on such topics as what an RV is, how to shop for one, and whether you are suited to the RV style. They also covered where to go during the winter and how to maintain various RV systems.

Although the couple originally was attracted to the camping lifestyle, their pop-up tent was not something a couple could live in full-time, Sandy says. "Alan thought we could," she says, "but it wasn't going to happen." As a result, the couple went right from a tent trailer to a fifth-wheel trailer, which Alan notes is a huge jump. "Most might go to a small trailer or pickup camper before they go into a big RV."

They learned at the Life on Wheels school that the average couple buys three RVs before finding the one that's the correct size for what they want to do. "I think we were able to do it in one step because we had done so much research and talked to so many people that we knew what we needed," Sandy says. Alan explains that the fifth-wheel trailer provides more living space "dollar for dollar per square foot" than a motor home. The downside: "It takes a little bit longer to set it up and take it down than a motor home."

The two did quite a bit of shopping for their RV. They visited several dealers—mostly in larger cities. They also went to several RV shows. "We learned as we went along," Alan said. The floor plan and construction quality—particularly the cabinets—were critical to their decision. "We both liked comfortable chairs," he says. "So we wanted to be sure we had two lounge chairs." The TV was not that important. Nor was a major entertainment center. "One thing we wish we had gotten that we did not is a desk of some kind."

Alan, who stands 6 foot 1, says he wanted to be certain that he could fit comfortably in the bed and shower. "We found at least three different sizes of queen-size beds," he says. "And some showers were difficult for me to get in and out of."

In the year before retiring, the couple spent $45,000 on their HitchHiker Premier wide-body fifth-wheeler. After casting off, they were forced to take interest from an annuity to finance an $80,000 international medium-duty truck.

Their 3354-foot fifth-wheel trailer has all the comforts of home on a down-sized basis. A fifth-wheel trailer hooks onto the bed of a truck and falls into a recreational vehicle category, in between a more expensive motor home and a standard trailer, which would be towed behind a car or sports utility vehicle. There is one bedroom and two "slide-outs," each extending the walls another 18 inches or so to allow for more room in the bedroom and the living room. The trailer already came with very heavy furniture. Custom features include carpeting on the ceiling for warmth and sound, heavy-duty brakes, special matching fabrics on the couches and chairs, and a smaller chair for the petite Sandy.

The rear of the trailer has a large wraparound bay window. "Making buying decisions is easy," Sandy says of her newer lifestyle. "We don't have space or the weight allowance, so we don't do impulse buying. We don't have a place to put it anyway."

Adds Alan, "It does create a challenge for families on birthdays and holidays. They have to consider the size and weight of anything they purchase." Alan explains that the manufacturer of the RV stipulates the amount of weight that the tires and axles can carry. Insurance companies that cover RVs are beginning to advise RV owners that they reserve the right to weigh the vehicle if the owner is at fault in an accident. If the vehicle is overweight, insurers might exclude coverage. So, the best gifts for their new lifestyle tend to be gift certificates, phone cards, and postage stamps—things they can use on their travels.

Initially, it was hard for family and friends to fathom that the two could leave everything behind and go off like that. Some probably thought they had lost their minds. "One of Alan's daughters thought we would drop off the face of the earth and she would never see us again," Sandy says.

Before selling their home, the couple invited their children to come and take anything they wanted. It made them feel very good to be able to give away their possessions at a fun time of their lives rather than in a crisis. "Plus," Alan says. "It's fun to visit them and see the things they took from us in their houses."

The direction the couple heads in their RV often depends upon the locations of their four grandchildren or an interesting article they've picked up in a newspaper.

The two keep a manila file for every state in the union and most of the Canadian provinces. As they read about interesting places in magazines and newspapers, they tear out the article and file it in the proper state so they know where to stop when they head that way. And Sandy keeps a travel log.

Alan remembers some of the interesting sites that made it into Sandy's log. There was the time they were driving in Nevada across the segment of U.S Highway 50, often dubbed, "The loneliest highway in America." Out in the middle of nowhere was an old dead cottonwood tree, with 200 or 300 pairs of shoes strung over it. But what took the cake on that same road was an extremely unusual piece of art. The body of an old Volkswagen Beetle had been mounted along the highway in somebody's yard. It was painted black and had huge 12-foot black legs that somebody had welded to it. Somebody evidently had tried to transform a VW Beetle from a little bug to a big black spider-like bug. "It just shows you," Alan says, "the creativity of America."

Yes, it can get lonely on the road, he says. "There are times when you miss those friends you used to spend a lot of time with. You miss your family, too. It's also nice to know when you wake up in the morning where in the world you are." Nevertheless, when they were campground hosts for the National Forest Service in Colorado, "a bunch of guys I used to work with in the real estate business came and spent a week with us," Alan says. "Those were people we knew before we got on the road."

Meanwhile, Alan says, he has gotten to see some incredible places that he otherwise might never have seen. Plus, their new adventure has presented an opportunity to meet new friends. For example, once at the Life on Wheels school, they parked next to a couple that, like them, had a fifth-wheel trailer. "We visited them at their home in Lancaster, California," Sandy says. The couple had a lot of property and let the Clarks stay in their RV for free while they were there. "That's the wonder of e-mail," Alan notes.

Fortunately, today even RV-ers can take advantage of e-mail and cell phones. The couple has a phone connection in their trailer but don't use it because most of the time they're not where a phone line is. Instead, they use a cell phone. They also have e-mail through a Sharp TM20. You can input e-mail, put it to a phone, and send and receive. E-mail messages are transmitted through PocketMail, which limits the number of characters they can contain and prohibits attached files. "We found that Internet access is not that easy," Alan says, noting that he's a bit sorry about that because he would like to get photos of his grandchildren. However, through PocketMail, the couple stays in touch with people several times a day. They use their daughter's address in Colorado as their official address.

***

Most of the Clarks' money is invested through a broker. When we talked with them, they had 30 percent in bonds, 15 percent in cash, and the rest in stocks. They also have a money market mutual fund, which lets them write checks against it and includes ATM access. Why so much in stocks? Long term, the couple says they need wealth to grow and keep up with inflation. Over the past three years, they saw the value of their stock investments decline. But their bonds appreciated in value.

Alan says of the couple's broker, "He's very good. We talk with him once a month to find out what our current cash position is and what our expenses for the next month are going to be." Sometimes the broker needs to adjust their investment positions accordingly.

When we interviewed them, Alan was less than one month away from collecting just over $1,200 monthly in Social Security. "If the market weren't in the tank, I might look at it a little differently," he says of the decision to collect Social Security at age 62 rather than wait for a larger $1,600-plus check at age 65. "But cash flow is important."

The Clarks often travel for three or four months at a time. When they expect to stay in an area for a while, they supplement their income with minimum-wage jobs for a maximum of four months.

The jobs give them some extra money and something to do. Yes, their assets have dropped a bit since the bear market took off in 2000, and both spouses were working a little more. However, they stress, they were not affected nearly as much as some of their friends.

"Last summer, we were at the National Forest Service for three months," Alan says. "We're not actually working where we are now, but we're helping Sandy's sister move into her house. We'll probably be here about four months.

"This next summer, normally, we would find a job for the summer. Our hope is that fuel prices won/t get too high and we will spend the summer traveling to Alaska, where we won't work."

The couple often uses "Work Kamper News" as a clearinghouse for job opportunities for RV-ers, although there also are other clearinghouses. They generally work in RV parks or campgrounds. Alan typically works on buildings and grounds in equipment maintenance; Sandy, who has a strong computer background, often works in the office or in retail sales.

They earn a mere $5 to $5.50 an hour each. "Sure you'd like to be making more money when you've earned more money before," Sandy says. But in their old jobs, they also spent more money. There were house payments and maintenance. There also were meals in restaurants and expensive clothes.

Meanwhile, even though their current pay may not be the highest, many of their costs are offset, Sandy says. They're saving on fuel costs and laundry. In an RV park, the park normally provides a site and hook-ups, which otherwise might cost anywhere from $15 to $30 per night. "Sometimes they make you work a certain number of hours to pay for it," Sandy stresses. Remuneration and benefits are negotiable.

"I have to say we have not had a problem finding work," Alan says. "People we know, for the most part, have very strong work ethics. I don't know too many of our acquaintances who have had any problem." Also, he notes, local newspapers are full of jobs. "You have to be very honest with potential employers and tell them you're only here for one month or six weeks or whatever period of time."

In a life previously filled with high pressure, the new jobs they are finding often are an educational experience. "You get to meet lots of different kinds of people," Alan says. "Some are doing the same thing you were. Others were a few years ago." In fact, they have met some of their best road friends while working. Take a couple they met in Benson, Arizona. The Clarks had been staying there three days, and just as they were pulling out, a man asked if they would be interested in working. They started the very next day and continued working there for three months. "They're the folks we're going to Alaska with," Sandy says.

While the Clarks' retired lifestyle meant giving up attractive incomes, they have substantially cut their costs. They estimate that their expenses run $3,000 monthly, compared with $5,000 monthly when they were living in a home. The $5,000 included some business expenses, Alan says.

"Things were a little bit more expensive than we had hoped," Alan acknowledges. "We were just thinking the other day that, had the stock market taken a dive in the spring of 2000 like it took in the last six or nine months, we might not have been so bold as to go out there. But since we're out there now full-timing, we have to find a way to make it work."

Although they are saving money living in an RV—including property taxes and yard maintenance costs—they had to shell out a lot of money to get started. After all, having the right machinery was essential.

Even though the Clarks have every convenience of home, they must watch expenses. They rarely eat out, but they enjoy libraries and museums that they find along the nation's back roads. And with the cost of fuel getting more expensive, they are currently limiting their travels to west of the Mississippi.

The cost of communications wound up being higher than when they were living in a stationary house. For one thing, they paid $100 for the e-mail device and still pay $149 annually for PocketMail. The cost of their cell phone is more expensive because they must have national coverage—a more expensive plan that costs $80 monthly. There's another $10 monthly charge for extra time on nights and weekends. In addition, they pay more in postage because they have their mail forwarded.

"One of the things that's hard to do when you travel is to take advantage of sales or coupons," Sandy adds. "We're never anywhere to get an ongoing paper. A lot of times we are in small communities where prices are higher for groceries."

They expect to ultimately save some money due to a solar heating system they installed in the trailer. "Last summer, when we lived in a very remote forest service campground, there was obviously no electricity," Alan says. "We were able to enjoy our microwave and TV because of the solar system we installed." Also, he notes, the solar system lets him avoid paying extra for electricity hook-ups at RV parks. It cost about $3,000 to install the solar system.

As with hotels, there are all types of places to park an RV. At least in the western part of the country, prices can run as high as $50 a night, according to Alan. The large, private resorts with swimming pools, cable television, and luxurious clubhouses charge the highest rates. "We don't want to have to pay for those amenities," Alan declares. "We can't afford the nicer RV parks, and a lot of times we're not in an area that has an RV park."

That's no problem, he says. 'There are lots and lots of places you can stay that are not in RV parks. He admits that lately they have been staying longer in places to avoid spending as much money on gas. Low-cost or even free places to stay may be state parks, national forests, or grounds owned by the U.S. Bureau of Land Management. Where they stop largely depends upon where they are when they're tired.

"There are a lot of people who stay in Wal-mart parking lots," Alan says. "Most Wal-mart stores will allow you to stay there one night. If you are a member of the Elks, they have low-cost parking close to their lodge." In fact, he says, lots of different organizations offer places to stay. But you don't necessarily want to go looking for a low-cost place ahead of time, he advises. That results in too much structure for your travel plans.

"What you need to do is figure out first where you want to go. Then, when you're tired, start looking in a general area for what's available. Sometimes it's a wide place on the road, a truck stop, or a rest area."

To save on places to park the RV, it is important to be "self-contained," Alan explains. "We've got our own water. We've got tanks to hold our own waste water. Plus, you can generate your own power as long as you've got batteries.

"In Lake Tahoe, we stayed in the parking lot of a casino," Sandy says. "They offered that capability." The two note that a number of publications list free and inexpensive areas to stay nationwide.

Because the Clarks paid cash for their truck and trailer, they have no monthly payments for those. They pay slightly less than $1,000 annually to insure their truck and trailer. The cost of truck repairs can be expensive. Although their overall cost of living appears lower in their newfangled style of retirement, some expenses were higher than they had anticipated.

It was particularly difficult when the couple first started, Sandy says. "We had terrible problems with our first truck." It had to be towed several times. For the first three weeks on the road, there was a mechanical problem virtually every day. Alan handles most of the maintenance on the road, and he was almost ready to give up. "It's frustrating," Sandy says. On the other hand, she stresses, some of the same types of frustrations come along with a house.

They admit that they are also fighting skyrocketing health insurance bills. At this writing, the two say that health insurance represented their highest monthly expense. As a result, they are self-insuring—with very high deductibles and paying $600 monthly for major medical health insurance.

Finding the right professionals can be tough while traveling. Fortunately, the health insurance plan they have provides a list of doctors in their geographic area. They just call down the list.

There is little the couple would change, and they have no plans to stop their traveling anytime soon. Will they do it forever? "Always is a long time," Alan says. "We certainly don't have any specific date as to when we might evaluate it or when we plan on stopping."

"We don't want to go back to having a house and working full-time," Sandy says firmly. "That seems like another world that we don't want to approach."

Doing it Yourself

If you're looking to go full-time in a recreational vehicle and would like to save money, now could be an attractive time to find a cheap vehicle, suggests Gaylord Maxwell, founder and president of the Life on Wheels school. That's because RV designs changed dramatically in the 1990s.

"The big change that occurred is the addition of slide-outs to the coach parts," Maxwell says. Today many RVs have slide-outs that let you increase the size of the vehicle as long as 13 feet. "This dramatically increases the floor space of the living room or dining area." Because of the change, persons whose RVs lack slide-outs are stuck with dinosaurs. "As trade-ins, they don't bring much," he says. "But if you're beginning this lifestyle and you want to economize, now is a good time to look at the used market." Often, he says, used RVs can be found parked in driveways with "for sale" signs on them.

On the other hand, he warns, don't fall into the trap of being too economy-minded that you buy something that isn't what you want. RVs can depreciate enormously. "If you buy a 40-footer with four slide-outs to begin with, then you never have to go back to anything else."

Shop around carefully for an RV loan, Maxwell suggests. Typically, they have a higher rate than a car loan, but the default rate is very low. You can find loans not only through banks or dealers, but also through major organizations, like the Good Sam Club, the largest club of RV owners.

Maxwell agrees that you can stay more cheaply at places such as the Wal-mart parking lot. "The bad thing that's happening is that people are staying more than one night." As a result, various jurisdictions are working to prohibit it; increasingly, signs are creeping up in Wal-mart parking lots banning overnight parking. Maxwell says he has seen such a sign in Yuma, Arizona. "I noticed people are there anyway overnight," he says.

"Most truck stops have parking areas that you can park in." Maxwell also says that you can park in Quartzsite, Arizona, for $125 a year. The U.S. Bureau of Land Management confirms that from September 15 through April 15, it charges $125 for seven months on its 11,400-acre long-term visitor area, just south of Quartzsite on Highway 95. But locals note that RV-ers often take advantage of free parking the rest of the year offered in conjunction with a host of large shows in that area. "The Bureau of Land Management provides dumpster services and portable toilets," Maxwell adds. Another way to save money: Visit children and friends, park in their driveways, and use their electricity. For free or low-cost places to park, visit www.freecampgrounds.com and www.publiclands.org.

Maxwell notes that today, you can buy an extreme variety of RVs. "Last year (2002), some of the bus conversion manufacturers put out a product that had price tags of just under $2 million," he says. "There are standard models made in excess of $1 million." You also can buy an RV for as little as $39,995, he said. "But that's a weekend rig that you go to the beach in or to a campground with the kids. That's not something that you go live in. For a motor home that would be large enough to live in, you're looking at more like $100,000."

You can buy a travel trailer for less, but that takes an expensive vehicle to pull it. 'You're still looking at $75,000 for a trailer and something to pull it in," he said. "You can spend a lot of money for these things, but you don't have to spend it."

Maxwell says that it's a known fact that everybody who goes full-timing in a recreational vehicle eventually stops at one time or another. For many, he says, it's due to health problems. "A lot just get tired of it. I don't have access to the people who get out of it. I don't see them.

"It used to be," he says, "that they miss the grandkids and family. I say to begin with, if you have to have your grandkids and kids around, it's not a lifestyle for you."

Nevertheless, he says, "the comment I have heard more than anything else as it pertains to finances about going full-timing is, 'If I had it to do over, I wouldn't have waited so long.' People have a preconceived notion. They feel they have to have more money than they have to have." Actually, he says, it largely depends upon what you're used to. "If you have more income in regular life, it takes more income in an RV life. If you're used to being poor, there's no reason to expect that you should live full-timing in a rich way. If you made $1,000 and you spent $1,002, it will be the same in RV-ing and full-timing."

There are some downsides to full-timing in an RV:
- Unlike homes, RVs depreciate rapidly in price. You can lose 20 percent of the value of the RV the first year you own it.
- You could have trouble finding places to park your RV during holidays or at popular tourist spots.
- If you want air-conditioning, you'll need a generator.
- You typically get low gas mileage with RVs—about 10 miles per gallon.
- Many garages lack space to repair RVs, and repairs can take much longer than with cars. It may take time to get the parts.
- You need to be careful that you don't run afoul of state or local regulation, such as those that restrict the size of your RV or govern where you may stop.
- You must drive slower with a heavier vehicle.

If you aren't sure whether to take the plunge, consider renting an RV to live in for less than $300 a month at some trailer parks. The *Miami Herald* reports that people on monthly incomes of $600 to $700 month can live comfortably in these parks. Not sure if traveling in an RV is for you? You can rent one for about $700 per week plus expenses, according to carbuyer.com.

Taking Social Security Early

Alan faced a dilemma sure to affect many retirees. Should he take Social Security early or postpone it to get more benefits? Alan decided to take his Social Security payments at age 62 instead of age 65 for good reason: He needed the money. He is not alone. Close to 70 percent of persons applying for social security are under age 65. But what if you don't necessarily need the money?

The bottom line is the longer you wait, the more you get each month. So you want to consider your own personal health. If you're going to postpone Social Security benefits, you want to be sure you'll still be around to collect them. You also want to consider how much in earnings you'll be giving up if you must tap into your savings to postpone Social Security benefits. The lower interest rates are, the less sacrifice you'll be making. It's a good idea to get a statement of your Social Security benefits to help you make this decision. You can get the information by calling the Social Security Administration at 1-800-772-1213, or writing to the Social Security Administration, Office of Earnings Operations, P.O. Box 33026, Baltimore, MD 21290. You also can also go to www.ssa.gov/mystatement to get the report.

Like an insurance actuary, you want to examine the added benefits you stand to receive by waiting to collect social security in relation to how long you expect to live. To help you with this, you can check life expectancy tables, known as the Commissioners 1980 Standard Ordinary Mortality Table, published in the *Life Insurance Fact Book*. You can purchase this table for $49.95 from the American Council of Life Insurance, 1511 Ritchie Highway, Arnold, MD 21012. Or, you simply can visit the public library or contact your insurance agent and ask what the life expectancy would be beyond the age you're considering collecting. Websites with life expectancy calculators include www.healthcentral.com and http://moneycentral.msn.com.

For example, let's say that a 55-year-old male who paid $43,651 into Social Security over the years wants to retire when he reaches age 62. The Social Security statement shows that if he collects at age 62, he would get $827 per month in social security. But by waiting until age 70, he would collect $1,462.

If the 62-year-old put off receiving Social Security for eight years, he would be minus a total of $79,392 in income ($827 a month for 96 months) by the time he reached age 70.

Although he would get $635 monthly more by waiting, will he live long enough to make up that lost $79,392? Of course, nobody knows for sure. But based on the 1980 Standard Ordinary Mortality Table, the average 70-year-old male has a life expectancy of another 11 years. Meanwhile, it would take about 10 years and 5 months for the retiree to make up this lost income ($79,392 divided by $635 is around 125 months, or almost 10.5 years.)

So this happens to be a pretty tough call. Once you see the hard numbers, only you can make the final decision.

Insurance That Your Money Won't Run Out

For added insurance that your money won't run out, you might consider investing in an immediate annuity. This is a contract with an insurance company. In return for a lump sum investment, you get a monthly check for as long as you live. However, once you invest in an annuity, you typically can't withdraw. This is starting to change, though. More insurance companies are letting you withdraw cash in emergencies if you agree to receive lower monthly payments.

An immediate annuity can be a good source of reliable income. You pay taxes only on the annuity's earnings. Be careful, though: Unless you make specific arrangements, an insurance company keeps the proceeds of the investment if you die before the money runs out.

With an immediate annuity, the most important thing is to check the financial strength of the insurance company that issues an annuity you're considering. Stick with the safest insurance companies rated at least A+ by A.M. Best or B+ by Weiss Ratings, Inc., and AA and Aa2 financial strength ratings by Standard 8c Poor's and Moody's, respectively.

It is easy to arrange for your heirs to get the proceeds of an annuity. One of the most common such contracts is called "10-year certain and life." Under this arrangement, you still get monthly checks for life. However, if you die within the first 10 years, the checks continue to your beneficiary until the 10 years are up.

Chapter 7

Victor and Ruth Barnard: Livening Up the Neighborhood

At 80 and 75, respectively, Victor and Ruth Barnard are the oldest residents in their neighborhood, dotted with some oddly colored homes—including a duplex painted half peach and half lavender. Then again, they were not looking for a conventional retirement. Nor did they find it. The couple, who say they have less than $250,000, helped pioneer a new economical lifestyle, called co-housing.

When they joined the core group that formed their 42-home community, Nyland Cohousing, in Lafayette, Colorado, it was one of just a handful of such projects in the country. Nyland was not tailored to senior citizens, nor is it a commune. Ruth Barnard stresses that residents are very careful to avoid the "commune" stigma. Nevertheless, the lifestyle marked quite a departure from their structured career backgrounds.

Ruth had been a teacher of art, learning disabilities, and behavior disorders. Victor was a lieutenant-colonel in the U.S. Air Force who served as an intelligence officer and tail gunner on a B-24 bomber during World War II. It was a second marriage for each, and together they have five grandchildren.

For Ruth, her newfangled retirement that started in 1988 initially meant having to deal with a radical element of the baby boomer generation, who viewed her as a parent. Victor, she says, had to learn not to give orders. They clearly were the aberration. Nevertheless, the two say they wouldn't change their unconventional lifestyle for the world.

"It's fun," Victor says of their lifestyle. "I enjoy it." Adds Ruth: "It's kind of like being in summer camp. You have a bunch of people around. We have fun. I'm pretty much an extrovert. Vic is more of an introvert. Neither of us wants to leave."

Fortunately, the couple had built up a little nest egg for their retirement years. Victor, having served in the U.S. Air Force for 30 years, had a generous government pension. Ruth had some stocks that she had inherited and never touched. "Merrill Lynch has been our holding place," she says, noting that they are careful not to take on too much risk. As a result, her investments, now in a living trust, grew in value. Their childhoods have influenced them to be frugal. The two were children of the Depression. "It means you don't spend a lot of money," Ruth declares. "We don't buy new cars. We've got a '96 Chevrolet Lumina. We just got it fixed for $1,000, but that'll last a while." Victor's car is a 1991 model. By living in a co-housing community, she adds, there is no pressure to impress anyone by spending money.

In the late 1980s, the Barnards were renting after moving from Illinois to Longmont, Colorado, and were looking for a place to buy. Victor saw an ad in the Boulder newspaper that said a core group was holding a meeting to form a new type of community that was common in Denmark.

The fact that the co-housing concept started in Denmark helped entice Victor. While in the military, he had been stationed in that country.

"My comment was, 'Ruth, if this thing started in Denmark, let's find out about it,'" Victor says. "The Danes were such nice people."

Being sociable people, the Barnards were attracted to co-housing because it fostered a positive people environment.

"I liked the fact that we would know our neighbors and have what I had when I was a kid and grew up in Gary, Indiana," Victor says. "No matter whether people spoke Polish, Hungarian, or German, you knew everybody. You helped out when they looked like they needed it. You were there for them, and vice versa."

Ruth says that when she was younger, neighbors never talked to one another to try to solve problems. "Once the woman next door was angry with my daughter," she says. "My daughter never told me that, so

I never got to solve the problem. Here we have mediation and all kinds of stuff—although it doesn't always work."

The couple attended the meeting at an area school, and Ruth, who had developed an interest in sociology, was very excited about the group's vision for an "intentional community." She also liked the fact that it was intergenerational. Residents were not limited to any particular age group.

After the meeting, Ruth asked Vic about the prospect of paying $5 for an introductory book on the subject. Victor's surprising response: "Aren't we going to buy a house?" The two were among the first to put down $1,000 toward the community.

The couple attended weekly meetings to plan the community for about two years before finally moving in around 1990. There were some heated discussions.

James Leach, who joined the group after it was further along and who now develops co-housing communities nationwide, recalls one that centered on what color to paint the houses.

"They had a color expert come in and recommend colors for their houses," he says. "A couple of people in the community decided they did not want to put up with someone telling them what color to paint their house."

The upshot of all the discussions: The color of your house is so subjective that you must get approval of the neighbors who would be looking at your house across the pedestrian ways. The result, he said, was everything from mauve to some really "bad greens that people picked."

Leach continues: "The color consultant got thrown out and all the recommendations got thrown out. "Some people were real proud of that. Others were kind of disgusted."

Ruth says that more recently, another color controversy was resolved. The decision: Roofs on the houses would be painted gray. It marked the end of discussions that had dragged on for a year. "Every meeting we had, somebody got up with a chart board," she says. "Finally, the roofers had to put the roofs on."

Although the group finally settled on gray, initially, some people in the community, including the Barnards, liked the idea of red tile. They were able to see the red tile roof of the University of Colorado from their home and admired it.

The problem: Some residents were angry at the University of Colorado for accepting defense grants and, thus, wanted nothing to do with anything that resembled the university. "These are peace and justice people," Ruth explains.

Leach recalls that, initially, financing development of co-housing communities was a problem. Banks had never heard of it. Meanwhile, some homes were as many as 300 feet from where residents parked their cars, and appraisers initially indicated that this lowered the value of the house.

"They wanted to know who these strange people were," Leach says. "It sounded like hippies. So we took Vic and Ruth and two or three other people who were a family with children. We went to the bank, sat right in front of the bankers and said, 'Here are your buyers.' They were normal folks who explained why they wanted to live in this kind of community. This got us to the point where we could finance the first community.

"The thing that convinced the lender was a combination of the fact that it wasn't as weird as it might look. They were real people. And we were an established development company partnering with them." The Barnards and a few other founding members actually signed on the construction loans so that the community could get off the ground.

The community, Leach adds, was one of the first to do recycling on a grand scale and to get the local regional transportation district to put in a bus stop there.

'The big difference is that it's resident-managed," Leach says. "You don't have outside managers. Residents are a lot more involved in the welfare of their neighborhood. It's pretty exemplary in terms of a grass-roots effort to raise our standards here and to raise the standards in the United States of how we live."

Like any housing subdivision, people in a cohousing community are free to buy and sell their homes for whatever price they want and to whomever they want. As with a homeowner's association or condo association, there also are monthly maintenance fees to cover the upkeep of the common areas and a board of directors to oversee the money. The Barnards, for example, paid $181 a month in maintenance fees for their

1,800 square-foot home. Meanwhile, residents pitch in to handle a lot of the services that otherwise would be handled by hired help.

"We have three community work days," Ruth says. The first one is in spring, which is for trimming, weeding, and making certain walkways are wide enough to accommodate fire trucks. There also are work days in June and September.

Unlike with condominiums or developments run by housing associations, the developer did not create Nyland. Rather, a core group of people, many loosely associated with the nearby University of Colorado in Boulder, got together and created it. They bought the land and hired an architect and builder. The group makes the decisions about landscaping and sets any rules.

Co-housing is designed to foster social activity. At the 40-acre Nyland Cohousing community, for example, there are no streets and few garages. Homes are founded on the principle that once you push a button on a garage door opener, you're never apt to see your neighbor. Instead, there are pedestrian ways, designed so that residents walk by the neighbors' homes and chat with people who might be sitting on the front porch. The pedestrian ways are U-shape, which Victor says "left us three nice big fields." The fields offer some 20 acres of open spaces. The Barnards walk past 15 houses to get to their home from their carport.

A 6,000-square-foot common house has two guest apartments. Meals are served at the common house tip to four days a week for just $3 per person per day. They are cooked by a three-member volunteer team.

There is a play area for children, garden areas where people grow vegetables adjoining a greenhouse, and a shop for residents to work on bicycles and cars.

"We see snow-capped mountains five or six months out of the year," Victor says of the community, located 6 miles outside Boulder. "Even in the summertime, the highest peaks look frosty."

Unlike condominium or housing developments, which typically come with 200-page books of sometimes-ridiculous legalese bylaws, the rules at Nyland Cohousing community are contained on four stapled pages. Although those rules were a long time in the making, they are very simple. Among the minimum criteria for community membership are the following:

Agreement to use only household products that are bio degradable and are easy on the septic systems and the land.
- Agreement that dogs should be on leashes. There also is a strong feeling among noncat owners that cats should be kept inside, where they cannot harm nesting birds and other wildlife.
- Each member is expected to actively participate in at least one "sustainment" group, which is involved in maintain ing one facet of the community.
- Community members must cook a "Common House meal every rotation." A rotation generally comes around every eight weeks.

At Nyland, the rules are few. No fines are levied if a rule is broken, either. If something bothers you, it's up to you to talk to your neighbor and get it resolved.

Although their development often is referred to as a "hippie commune," the Barnards claim that it is quite different from a commune. Most of the residents are professionals, although Ruth says they are not necessarily the richest professionals. They tend to be therapists, computer workers, and engineers. One resident is a pediatrician, she notes, but he got so sick of the HMO he worked for that he just quit. "Now he's just being a Buddhist."

"Quite a few are vegetarians," Ruth says of the residents. "But if a good fish meal comes along, you'd be surprised at the number of people who sign up. If a meal is good enough, they eat meat."

According to Ruth, the Nyland Cohousing community claims to have three objectives: economy, ecology, and cooperation. So far, the Barnards believe the community has helped them economize. The couple has less than $250,000 in assets. But county records indicate that the Barnard's house, which they paid $128,000 for, is now worth at least $250,000.

The two have no mortgage. Together, their annual pension and Social Security incomes total about $64,000, so their monthly income is plenty to live on.

Fortunately, the Barnards don't have to worry about health insurance. Ruth has Medicare and a secondary insurance policy from her teaching career.

Recently, however, the U.S. Air Force has began offering a program called TRICARE for Life. Once they turn 65 years old, beneficiaries are required to purchase Medicare Part B and pay those premiums. However, TRICARE picks up the rest of the coverage, with no enrollment fee. Ruth says she is considering dropping her secondary coverage.

Aside from their health benefits, the Barnards say they have found co-housing a very affordable way to own a home. The reasons include these:

- There are group dinners at the common house four days per week. They spend just $3 per person per meal or $24 dollars a week for four communal meals. That represents a savings of a couple of hundred dollars a month if they had to buy the food and prepare the meals at home. If they went out to dinner four nights a week, it would cost them over $140 a week, or a whooping $560 per month.
- They pay a monthly maintenance fee. This saves them several hundred dollars a year, compared with the expense of living in a standalone home. They say residents also volunteer their services at lower cost. For example, the Barnards pay a maid $20 an hour to clean their house.
- The electricity bills in the home are cheap due to environmentally friendly construction of the houses, which share common walls with neighbors. Walls are insulated with wet-spray cellulose made mostly from recycled paper. The Barnards estimate that they save about 25 percent over the cost of electricity when they owned a home in Illinois.
- Front yards are xeriscapes, which they claim use less water and are easier to maintain. Xeriscapes can cut water usage in half. They carefully consider the appropriate plants for the area as well as the soil and turf. They also make use of efficient irrigation techniques, mulches, and appropriate maintenance procedures.
- The complex has a solar-heated greenhouse. Residents often donate vegetables seeded in the greenhouse for cooking communal meals. The cost of the greenhouse is kept low through community projects.

- Money that the residents earn through activities is set aside in a separate corporation to help finance necessities for the common elements, such as new chairs and carpets for the common house, cutting homeowners' costs.

Ruth calls the group a "family." When it started, she says, the core group was made up of hippies, and many had lived in communes. "They didn't want any kind of governmental stuff," she says. "We've become a lot stronger as we've grown because we've found out that you do have to have insurance. You do have to have funds that you can paint your houses with."

Many of the original founders were dreamers, she says. In fact, she says that many of the more radical members who refused to listen to the other residents' needs finally moved out. At Nyland, everybody has a say in what gets done.

"Nobody gives anybody any power," she says. "Therein lie some of the sociological troubles. We didn't want to have anyone more powerful than anybody else."

Idealistically, the political setup at Nyland seems great. Unlike condominium associations, there are no "condo commandos" issuing rules or ordering people around.

But in reality, there are disagreements.

Take the neighbor whose house has one level that is an aquamarine shade of blue, another turquoise, and the top floor painted lighter turquoise with, as Ruth puts it, "a sickly green trim." When it was planned, residents were asked to say what colors they wanted their house. These neighbors had given their opinion and made a model of it. "We had a chance to say we feel it's a little too bright," she says. Some 20 notes were left on the house by residents who expressed how they felt about it. To this day, the house stands in full glory painted in those bright colors—despite the protests. The opponents simply have learned to live with it.

Then there was the case of a barking dog. The dog would go outside through a dog door into the yard and bark, howl, and cry. That problem was successfully resolved in mediation. The owners agreed to build a stairway from the basement level so the dog could go up the stairs and be with the residents rather than annoy neighbors. And there was the case of the neighbor who decided to extend a porch onto common land, which is owned equally by the 42 owners of the co-housing community. That issue never was resolved, Ruth says, and the community simply decided to live with it and grandfather the porch.

Then again, there are positive community events. For example, about a week or so after we first interviewed the Barnards, bagels were slated to be served at a meeting designed so that residents could discuss their vision for child care.

Also, all are pitching in to help one resident who was to go through chemotherapy. Residents were penning their names on a sign-up list to take turns bringing her food.

Then there was the resident who lived in Nyland part-time. She recently died. "We had meetings with her to say good-bye and had meetings afterward to give everybody a sense of what Dorothy meant to us," Ruth says. "This kind of acceptance of what's happening in other people's families is really very important."

There also are fun activities for the residents of the complex. One issue of the "Nyland News," a community newsletter, offered a monthly calendar of events that included yoga and Zimbabwean music in the commons. Another honored Victor with a "Great Job Golden Gloves" award for: "His command performance on the field of land-use workdays," his "daily ongoing and valiant battle against the enemy weeds in the community landscape," and his background "as an ex-military officer graciously living with a bunch of draft dodgers."

The award was presented with the recognition that living at Nyland "is a voluntary endeavor filled with the greatest dangers, including being known as that colorful neighbor in Lafayette, being known as that middle-age hippie commune, and being known as that gated liberal community without gates."

The Barnards are getting up in years. Stairs in the community are becoming harder to navigate. They initially told us that they were contemplating trading their lifestyle for a continuing-care facility in Colorado Springs, where Ruth's daughter is located. There also are three military hospitals in that area.

In Colorado Springs, Victor had explained, he would have many benefits as a retired military officer. He could shop at the post exchange, go to the commissary, belong to the officer's club, and use the golf courses and swimming facilities. "It's like having your own country club, but you don't have to pay for it."

While there is no military hospital near Nyland, there are hospitals in Colorado Springs.

Continuing-care facilities are not nursing homes or assisted-living facilities. Most important, though, there are nurses on duty 24 hours a day. Medical doctors may have offices in or near the facility.

People live independently in their own apartments. They pay a monthly fee that includes rent, meals, and often housekeeping. There may be transportation provided so that residents don't have to drive. Plus, some facilities go so far as to have a small grocery store, dry cleaner, bank, drugstore and beauty parlor/barber shop on the premises. There may be guest speakers, musical groups, book discussion groups, bingo, and movies. Often daily group activities promote exercise and interaction among people.

Generally, there are elevators to get the upper-level apartments, something that is conspicuously missing from Nyland. Ruth says that there are plans to put elevators in Nyland's common house, but it likely won't happen for several years because the next oldest residents are only in their 50s. They are not yet concerned about it. Newer co-housing communities are more careful to construct them in a senior-friendly way from the beginning.

Because continuing-care facilities include meals, they can be more expensive than living alone. But the Barnards figure that once they sell their house, they should be comfortable.

Ruth initially told us that she was slowly starting to give away the books in her house in preparation for the move.

"We won't have to do the cooking ourselves," Ruth said. "We have not yet gone to Colorado Springs to investigate it. But I'm a planner. We want to have things planned ahead and not have a crisis."

However, in a subsequent interview, her tone had changed. Ruth informed us that it's quite possible that they might stay at Nyland. The catalyst might have been a birthday party a couple of women in the community had for them as Victor celebrated his eightieth birthday and Ruth turned 75. "One of the women, in charge of the party said, 'Ruth. I'm going to warn you. I'm going to do everything in my power to keep the two of you here,'" Ruth recounts.

More recently, a group of women in the community had gotten together. "They wanted to know what they could do here in the community to help us," Ruth says. "They don't want us to leave."

Although many of the residents, in their baby boomer years, had been resistant to the idea of adding elevators to the buildings, Ruth says that they finally might be starting to see the light. "So we're staying and trying to figure out what it is we need. My daughter is relieved. She has three children to raise."

Doing It Yourself

You can cut your living costs through a variety of different living arrangements. Co-housing, which the Barnards experienced, is just one example.

There are some 68 co-housing communities nationwide and more than that number under development, according to the Cohousing Network in Oakland, California. For more information, visit the network at www.cohousing.org.

Co-housing groups collectively own land, says Laird Schaub, executive secretary for the Fellowship for Intentional Community in Rutledge, Missouri. However, each individual privately owns his or her own home. Typically, there is a homeowner's association fee to cover upkeep of joint property, and liabilities are jointly shared.

Housing almost always is clustered, and buildings typically face each other, to encourage contact among neighbors. Often there's a large amount of jointly owned open spaces and a jointly owned common house. Sometimes there is a shop in the basement and laundry facilities. There may be swimming pools, saunas, and hot tubs. Generally, the homes are smaller and the owners are living on the basis of explicit common values.

Schaub advises that if you're considering co-housing, you should ask how clear the group is about what it means to be a member. Too often, he says, an architect or developer is aggressively selling what sounds like a great concept. But once people get into the community, they might have different perceptions. One member might expect nightly communal dinners, for example. Another might expect dinners just monthly. It's best to iron out some of these issues before you buy into it.

Another important thing to find out is how the co-housing members work through disagreements. "It's easy enough to identify the advantages," Schaub says, "but what happens if two residents disagree?" You need to determine how disagreements are worked out, whether through a committee, a leader, or majority rule.

Commune-Style housing

Co-housing may be the newest and one of the hottest forms of "intentional communities," but it is not the only one. Perhaps more common are commune-style arrangements. With these arrangements, money earned by individuals belongs to the group. In some cases, the group may also own assets.

Many types of intentional communities are spiritual. Some might follow a particular spiritual path, such as a Buddhist ashram. Others simply promote general spiritual development.

Although there are many other intentional communities that have no spiritual basis, Schaub says that in any of these communal types of arrangements, you can expect various forms of income sharing. In some cases, all the money, including assets, may go to the group. In others, you just need to provide income. Yet others might have partial income arrangements.

Schaub suggests that some of the most important questions to ask of most such commune-style arrangements are these:

- Who owns the property? For example, is it the developer, a religious guru or the residents?
- What rights do you have to use the land? Can you plant a garden on it? Can you build an addition to your room if you'd like?
- What rights do you have in the decision-making about its use as a member? Do you have a direct vote? Does a board of directors vote? Or is there one charismatic leader make the decisions?
- Does the community have children? If you have younger children, you might prefer that children be allowed in the community. On the other hand, if you're a retiree, perhaps you'd prefer that there are no children.

- What contributions of dollars or labor are expected of you? Determine whether you must pay a monthly or periodic maintenance fee or whether you must obtain contributions from strangers to help the community function.
- What level of engagement is expected from members? Schaub says he knows of some communities that require meetings daily. "That's extreme. Other groups meet monthly for a pot-luck dinner. "There's a wide gap in the level of engagement."
- What happens as people get older? What provisions have been made—not only economically, but also physically, as capability is diminished? Do the requirements that you prepare a common meal or provide other labor diminish? In some cases, he says, you might be able to arrange to provide money in lieu of service.

"Don't go out and sell your house before going and visiting the community," Schaub adds. "A weekend or weeklong visit is cheap compared with spending lots of money." You can learn more about intentional communities by visiting his nonprofit organization's website at www.ic.org. The organization also publishes a listing of more than 600 "intentional communities" for $30.

Shared-Living Residence Program

In these residences, three or more unrelated people live in one home, have their own bedrooms, and share common areas, such as the kitchen, dining room, and living room. Management and maintenance of the home are decided mutually. These residences can be older converted homes, which may have shared bathrooms or steps, or brand-new shared residences. Often they are subsidized by federal, state, or local agencies.

Marjorie Marlin, executive director of the Cooperative Housing Corp. in Somerville, New Jersey, suggests that anyone considering group housing follow these tips:

- Try to go into a facility that's licensed. This, she says, "insures they're operating at a minimal standard that's been set up by the agency that licensed them. It means they're inspected.

- Find out which services are included and which aren't. "Every place should have a policies and procedures man ual." Is smoking allowed? Are pets allowed? Are cars allowed? You want to know some of these things.
- Determine whether well-known area agencies are aware of the facility you are considering. If it is reputable, chances are, your area office on aging, local churches, temples, or the visiting nurses association might know about it. "If they're totally unaware of the existence of a place, I would be concerned," she says.

The National Resource and Policy Center on Housing and Long Term Care warns that if you are considering any type of shared housing arrangement, you should first check local zoning ordinances. There could be local restrictions on housing meant for single-family homes. Sometimes the definition of "family" may prevent you from sharing a home, it says. Also, the agency warns, some areas do not recognize shared housing agreements as legitimate landlord/tenant contracts.

In addition, the agency warns that reduced rent or food might be considered income, affecting Supplemental Security Income benefits. "You may lose up to one third of your monthly benefits if the shared housing arrangement involves the exchange of reduced rent or food," it says. You also could lose food stamp benefits. The agency suggests checking with your insurance company. It's possible that a shared housing arrangement also might increase your local taxes or insurance rates.

Match-Up Programs

Under this type of program, a person with a house and extra room gets matched up with another person looking to rent space. There may be a fee or suggested contribution to the agency that arranges the match. "We find that clients get along better with each other if there is an age difference than when two people of the same age live together in a home," notes Rita Zadoff, co-president of the National Shared Housing Resource Center in Atlanta.

Persons considering this program need to be ready to agree on furniture arrangements. For example, some of the available existing homes already are furnished, so prospective tenants may not be able to move in their own furniture. Also, Zadoff warns, food issues need to be ironed out. "Many like to share food, but today we are all on different diets. Some people work it out without any problems. Some do not want to work it out with someone else."

For more information on shared-living residence programs and match-up programs, which total some 350 nationwide, visit the National Shared Housing Resource Center, at www. nationalsharedhousing. org.

Accessory Units

Another way to cut costs is to rent an apartment or a small home adjacent to an existing family home. This way, the homeowner, who may or may not be a member of your family, can earn rent from you. Meanwhile, you can pay a modest rent and still live independently.

Or, if you already own a home, you might want to add an apartment or home to rent out as a means of obtaining additional income. According to the National Resource and Policy Center on Housing and Long Term Care, accessory apartments can run $20,000 or more. Complete, portable small homes installed in the back or side yards of single-family lots can run at least $30,000.

The agency advises that if you consider an accessory unit, you explore local zoning ordinances and, if necessary, secure a "conditional" or special use permit. Make certain that no conditions or "covenants" written into the deed could hinder your efforts. You also should inform neighbors and neighborhood associations of your plans, to make certain there are no objections. And consult with a tax adviser to find out any impact that renting an accessory unit might have on taxes or your eligibility for public programs.

If you're the one building the unit, you'll need to apply for necessary permits and determine whether you can afford the time and expense involved. Be certain that any contractor you consider is licensed and bonded. Make only a small down payment. Pay only when the property is completed.

It may be possible to get federal funding for a type of accessory apartment, known as an ECHO, or Elder Cottage Housing Opportunity unit, which is designed to be temporary. However, warns a spokesman for the U.S. Department of Housing and Urban Development, "the problem is local zoning restrictions often don't permit this type of housing."

Nationwide, there are some 350 shared-housing programs. For the following shared-housing programs, you can visit the National Shared Housing Resource Center, at www. nationalsharedhousing.org, for more information.

Chapter 8

Alejandro "Alex" and Letty Monforte: Immigrants Parlay Job Benefits into the Good Life

Today Alejandro "Alex" Monforte, 66, drives only American cars. It is a deliberate tribute to the country that gave him an opportunity after he came over from the Philippines with just $100 in his pocket. When he was 59/4 years old, Alex, who originally left his wife and young child to travel to this country in search of a better economic opportunity for his family, made yet another bold move: He retired early.

Alex had been earning $100,000 as a procurement officer for the United Nations Children's Fund (UNICEF) in New York City. Yet, six months before he turned 60—the official retirement age for UNICEF, the father of three decided to quit. By failing to wait an additional six months, he deliberately chose to give up $1,200 in annual retirement income. Instead, he moved to Beverly Hills, Florida, where his retired wife, Letty, 67, already was living.

Although the Monfortes are stretching their money, the two live very comfortably in a three-bedroom house, with a lanai and swimming pool, on two wooded acres. They credit a relatively simple lifestyle, including a move to a lower-cost area, for their successful retirement.

The cars the Monfortes drive are not the fanciest. "Right now, we have a 1990 Buick LeSabre and a 1997 Ford Explorer," Alex says. "I never bought a car made in other countries— except my first car was a Volkswagen. That was the only car I could afford at the time." The Monfortes don't travel much, except largely to visit family members.

The Monfortes first met in the Philippines. Alex was born in Legaspi in the province of Albay. When Alex was about 5 years old, he lived through the horror of knowing that the Japanese ultimately would be coming to his hometown. Nobody knew what they would do. "We were all afraid," he says.

As it turned out, the Japanese occupied virtually every town. He remembers that they took over his school and forced him to do calisthenics. But fortunately, his family owned a home in the countryside. The word was if you lived in the countryside, you could easily survive. "It was like 100 percent guaranteed because you can just go into the forest and pick some vegetables that you could eat. Or, you could go fishing in the lakes or rivers. (We had) relatives there. They usually helped each other. If you wanted to borrow a sack of rice, you could borrow a sack of rice. We did not go hungry."

Alex's father was a bookkeeper, and his mother was a dressmaker. He lived with one brother and five sisters. "We were taught some Japanese words. I still remember some of the words I learned." Once in school, however, Alex no longer feared the Japanese. The problems were in the mountains some 25 miles away, where guerillas were fighting.

"As a matter of fact, we became friendly with two Japanese soldiers," he says. "They used to come to our house on Sunday afternoon. My mother would cook some food and they would partake with us in our dinner.

"What's so funny is, when the Americans came back to the Philippines and drove out the Japanese, the same thing happened. We became friendly with the Americans and my mother cooked food for them. I said, 'Gee, these guys are all human beings—even though they're the enemy. But, you know. They're away from home. They're lonely. They're trying to find some friends.'"

It was very fortunate that Alex and Letty's families resided in the countryside. Based on historic reports, other Filipinos truly suffered under Japanese rule. Published reports indicate that Filipino women were enslaved and forced to have sex with men in the Japanese army. Some women, delirious with malaria, were beaten and threatened with death. People were dissected without anesthesia for biochemical experiments. Filipino men and American soldiers were beaten and often beheaded. And in 1946, when Gen. Douglas MacArthur liberated the island, 19,000 Japanese soldiers under Vice Admiral Sanji Iwabuchi massacred 100,000 Filipinos before they were captured by U.S. forces.

Someone seemed to be looking after the Monfortes. And the family subsequently made the best of their opportunities.

When Alex first came to San Francisco, he had one daughter. Two more soon were on the way. Now all three daughters are married and on their own.

But while working in sales promotion in Mobil Oil in the Philippines, Alex realized that the economy in that country was holding the family back.

"I would not say it was bad," he says of his own personal plight. "The problem was we already had one child. Both my wife and I were working, but our salaries were just enough. We had no savings whatsoever. We were renting an apartment."

Alex's boss at Mobil Oil already had moved to the United States, and the two had been corresponding in the late 1960s. He was an engineer and had been hired by the city of Seattle. His old boss helped plant the idea of coming to the United States.

Alex also began talking to his brother-in-law about moving to the United States. Finally, his brother-in-law made the move. An artist, he found work in a San Francisco art gallery. So, with just enough money for airfare, Alex temporarily left his wife and child and moved to San Francisco. Fortunately, he already knew English.

"While I was looking for a job, (my brother-in-law) got me to work in the gallery temporarily." It was not exactly what he was trained to do. Alex had graduated from University of the East in Manila, where he had studied accounting and marketing. His first job in the United States paid only minimum wage. Largely, he showed paintings to the customers, nailed paintings into frames, and put them on a corrugated board and wrapped them in twine so that customers could carry them home. At first, finding a higher-paying job in his field was difficult.

Nevertheless, Alex, who always kept in touch with old friends, located a former co-worker from Mobil Oil, who had come to the United States. "First, she went to Canada and it didn't work out."

The former co-worker had been hired by UNICEF and suggested that Alex come to New York City. She would help him apply for work.

In February 1969, Monforte left San Francisco for New York City on a Greyhound bus with just $250. It was a trip he'll never forget. He had no place to stay, and he could not stay with his friend from Mobil Oil because she had female roommates.

So, he contacted an old high school buddy he knew had been living alone in New York alone. Alex was able to stay with him temporarily. He was expected to arrive Saturday evening. As it turned out, however, his friend was unable to pick him up that night. Alex had to stay at a YMCA, which, at the time, cost an astronomical $20 per night.

The next morning, Alex was in for another shock. He woke up to one of New York's historically worst snow storms, which had dumped more than 25 inches in some areas of the city. To make matters worse, areas went unplowed for a week because much of the city's snow-removal equipment had been buried. It was quite an inauguration for someone whose experience with snow largely had been limited to Christmas cards.

"All the restaurants were closed," he says of the New York fiasco. "You could hardly walk on the sidewalk. All the cars were covered with snow."

As it turned out, his friend could not pick him up for four more days, and Alex was unable to go anywhere. His money was rapidly running out. Finally, his old high school friend picked him up and took him to UNICEF so he could apply for a job.

There he found that his former Mobil Oil co-worker had been friendly with the personnel officer. Alex passed the required test, but initially his prospects were bad. "The accounting manager told me there were no openings. They would keep my papers on a file and would contact me if a job comes up."

Dejected, Alex was on his way out to lunch with his friend when the personnel officer came running to tell him that the accounting manager wanted to talk to him one more time. He had just remembered that one of the other UNICEF divisions had been looking for an accounting clerk who could type.

At the time, there were no computers, so typing was an important skill. Checks had to be typed on a typewriter. Fortunately, it was a skill that Alex had. He finally was hired as an accounts payable clerk at a salary of $6,000 annually.

Once Alex found a job, his old high school friend told him he could not stay with him because he was not allowed to have a roommate. Because Alex knew no one else, he checked into yet another YMCA. "I think I stayed there for like a week. Then I was able to get in touch with another former co-worker from Mobil Oil. He was working for Pan Am and knew of some Filipinos who were looking for one more roommate in Brooklyn. I got in touch with the guys, and they took me in."

Finally, more than five months later, Alex was able to send for Letty and their daughter. They arrived in August 1969; the United Nations arranged for their visas. While waiting, Alex found an apartment directly across the street from where he had been staying.

Initially, life wasn't easy at the United Nations. There were no benefits for clerical workers. Fortunately, his upbringing in Catholic school not only had made him independent, but also taught him better English than most foreigners spoke. Plus, his Catholic upbringing as an altar boy and ultimately work as a catechism teacher fostered independence. He began hearing that once you become a "professional" at the United Nations, you could be eligible for some attractive benefits.

Some of those benefits, he now admits, were instrumental in financing his attractive retirement. Although Alex had been aware of the benefits, it was not easy making it to the professional level. He was shy. "I worked very hard. I did what I was expected to do. I gave 110 percent." While he won't say that he stayed late every night, he acknowledges that he never wasted his time. "I always followed orders from my supervisors. I did not cross them."

Alex says he never actually applied aggressively for a higher-level job. The pieces just seemed to fall into place. First, he says, a clerk had left a job that was one level higher than his. "After she quit, my boss asked me if I wanted her job. I said 'Yes.'" The job was in inventory accounting. The procurement officer often came to examine inventories that they were using in the manufacture of UNICEF greeting cards to ensure that there were adequate supplies of materials. "He was satisfied with all the information I supplied him. Anytime he came to me, I gave him what he wanted."

Finally, the procurement officer's assistant left to get married. Alex was offered the job. "At first I said, 'What would the job offer me?' The response: 'A chance to become a professional.'"

Those were some magic words. It was his chance to get some nice benefits. Initially, Alex advised the procurement officer to talk it over with his boss. His own supervisor, along with the procurement officer, finally went to a higher-up that oversaw both their jobs. The final result: "If it's good for Alex, I have no objections," their supervisor had said. Alex finally had reached his goal.

Once Alex moved into the professional level, the family was able to afford a home in Long Island. In addition, professional benefits very conveniently included payment for 75 percent of his children's education, from kindergarten through college. That was a great financial boost with three children in tow.

When his boss moved away, Alex finally was named procurement officer.

***

Although Alex finally was making a comfortable salary, he was not enjoying his work. It became worse when his former boss, who already had taken early retirement, no longer was around to protect him. He had retired just months before Alex. But unlike Alex, his boss had more years under his belt and was able to claim more in the way of retirement benefits.

Rather than assuming that his net worth would suffer by retiring early, as many might, Alex decided to seek the hard figures. "I went to my pension plan office and asked how much I would be getting if I retired in May 1997 as opposed to December 1996," he says. "They said there would be $100-a-month difference."

Letty, already retired, was living in Florida. "I called my wife and told her about it. She said, 'The decision is yours. If you can't stand it anymore, then leave.'"

It was a difficult decision. By retiring six months early, he was giving up $100 monthly in extra retirement income, when he knew he would be living on a fixed income for years to come. "I was afraid I was going nuts," Alex says of his brazen move. "I thought the $100 monthly (in extra retirement benefits) wouldn't be worth it if I ended up in the hospital."

Alex began to earn a six-figure income only in the last few years of his job. In the meantime, he had been living in one of the highest-cost areas of the country. If the family had lived in the Midwest or in southeastern or western states, his final paycheck might have been equivalent to $50,000 a year.

Fortunately, through some excellent timing and insight on the part of Letty Monforte, Alex already had his impressive retirement home awaiting him.

The Florida real estate recession in 1991 was near the bottom. A friend of the couple had informed him that a Realtor from Florida had wanted to show them some lots. "He asked me if I wanted to come. The deal was that we would fly from New York Friday evening. They would meet us, pick us up, and put us in a condominium, at no charge to us. Plane fare coming here would be shouldered by the Realtor. If we decided to buy a lot, the Realtor would pay our return fare. Otherwise, it would be shouldered by us."

That weekend, the Monfortes, among four couples who took the trip, were shown all available lots. They had no intention of buying. But when the Realtor showed the couple one wooded corner 2-acre lot, Letty Monforte fell in love.

"We were the first ones to buy," Monforte says. "My wife has very good instinct. I let her make the decision."

The $30,000 lot, which sounded awfully cheap when compared with real estate in New York, came with water lines, telephone lines, and electricity.

It was nearly three years later before the couple actually built their home. Although they had planned to wait, they began noticing that prices were rising. So they finally decided to hire a builder and use it for a nice vacation home. The cost to build their dream home: another $130,000.

"We picked the model. We made different changes."

Between the couple's pensions and Letty's Social Security check, the two earn $40,000 annually, or an average of $3,333 monthly, in retirement. Plus, they gross $1,200 monthly in rent from their three-bedroom home in Long Island. They pay maintenance costs, insurance costs, some $3,600 in annual property taxes on their Long Island home. Plus, in Florida, there are $1,400 in property taxes and $99 in annual maintenance for the clubhouse, tennis courts, and roads. Alex also pays $165 monthly for his health insurance, and Letty pays for Medicare.

When they retired, they had $250,000 in savings. This included a third of Alex's pension—about $200,000, which he opted to take up front and invest in mutual funds. The couple also saved another $50,000, left over from Letty's job as an accounting clerk with Chase Manhattan Bank.

Fortunately, the mortgage on the couple's Long Island ranch house, which they originally purchased in 1976 for $42,500, is paid off. Since their retirement, the couple refinanced their mortgage on their Florida home and have just $94,000 left to go. Because Alex's holdings were well diversified in mutual funds, he says he has not been hurt terribly by the bear market of the previous three years.

Alex and Letty walk 2 miles each morning. Alex plays tennis four times a week—twice playing singles and twice playing doubles.

Tennis, Alex notes, is not an expensive sport—especially when your development makes tennis courts available for free.

"It's not like golf. With golf, you have to be a member. The fees are too high. My other sport is target-shooting. I read in the papers about this class on self-protection. I joined it. We met four times." At the last session, which focused on shooting, Alex learned about his shooting club. "We were asked to join. My wife goes to yoga every Wednesday morning, so she has friends over there."

He also volunteers for a neighborhood crime watch program around his development, and he drives a car owned by the Citrus County (Florida) sheriff's office. It has a two-way radio.

"We live a very simple life," Alex says. "We don't go out to eat. My wife, for one, is a good cook. I did not marry an expensive wife." Letty, an antique-lover, goes shopping at flea markets. She used to go to auctions.

While medical insurance is a problem for many, it is not a major issue for the Monfortes. While they worked, Letty was covered under Alex's medical and dental insurance. He still qualifies for coverage under that same plan at a reduced rate.

Alex says he sees absolutely no downside to retirement.

"What I can see is that people who didn't plan their retirement are having a hard time: people who don't have friends— people who keep to themselves. Those are the people who are not having fun."

Fortunately, Alex always had friends to help him through life. It's not that he is overly aggressive, although he admits that living with a large family gave him quite a bit of experience in dealing with people. "When somebody starts talking to me, then I can continue the conversation. I'm able to do that.

"When I arrived in the United States, people were friendly. When we were renting an apartment in Brooklyn, we wanted to get out of the city on weekends. We went camping with a tent, which we loaded on top of the Volkswagen practically every weekend. One thing we noticed at the camp sites was that because people are so relaxed and having a good time, people were friendlier.

"I know some people, for example, who think they are being discriminated against because they are not white Americans. In my case, I never experienced that."

Even where he currently lives, Alex says, everybody says hello to each other. Friendliness not only was critical throughout his life, but it is especially important in retirement. Spending time with good friends can prove a very inexpensive pastime.

To those who would like to retire early, Alex advises not eating out as much—only on occasions. "Because, boy, it's very costly." If two of you eat out three times a week at a modestly price restaurant (a $10 total bill), it can cost over $1,500 a year.

Another piece of advice: Always try to buy your home; don't rent. "If you are renting all the time, the money you spend for rent is not going anywhere except to the owner of the property you're renting from." Alex estimates that his small ranch house in Long Island today is worth about $250,000, representing an almost sixfold increase in value over the years.

Alex also believes that although you might hire people to handle maintenance around your home when you are working, there is no reason to do it when you retire. After all, time is much less scarce. 'Just the other day, my wife asked me to reupholster some furniture—some chairs from the flea market. We don't hire anybody to do those things. We only hire somebody to repair the pump of the pool when something goes wrong, or the air-conditioner."

Most of the tasks they do around the house are self-taught. Letty often watches HGTV and Martha Stewart. She provided the directions on how to upholster the chair: Simply remove the screw that holds the seat, and staple the material with a staple gun, the two figured out.

If you learn to repair things around the house and take care of the yard, you can save a couple of thousand dollars a year. By doing things yourself, it can prove much easier to live on a fixed income when the cost of goods and services is rising.

Alex says that while he is thankful for the opportunities given to him in this country, he admits that it could be harder for someone today to achieve as much as he has.

For one thing, he notes, it is critical that anyone immigrating to this country have a valid visa. It's much tougher now than when he came to this country cold. "Employers who employ people without green cards are being penalized by the government," he notes. "Very few companies take the risk."

Even today, Alex's advice to an immigrant seeking a better life is not necessarily to strive for the best benefits. "Grab the first job that's available, and start looking around once you have a job," he suggests.

"A lot of people jump from one company to another. By the time they retire, they have nothing." If you're already working, he advises that it pays to stick with one company.

Doing It Yourself

Unfortunately, because of changes in immigration laws, it's no longer as easy to immigrate to the United States as it was when Alex came to this country in the 1960s. To get to the United States today, prospective immigrants must have either a temporary or a permanent visa. Permanent visas are also known as green cards.

You can get a permanent visa in three ways, says Stephen Yale-Loehr, who teaches immigration law at Cornell University in Ithaca, New York:

- You can apply to a green card lottery. « An employer may sponsor you.
- A close family member may sponsor you.

Applying to the Green Card Lottery

Through the green card lottery, 50,000 immigrants are randomly selected annually to come into the United States. Set up by the U.S.

Congress in the early 1990s, the lottery is designed to be fair to those who don't have close family members or employers to sponsor them for immigration into the United States. "Almost anyone can apply for the lottery—except if they come from a country that already sends a lot of immigrants to the United States," Yale-Loehr explains.

Each year, the U.S. State Department lists certain countries from which immigrants cannot apply. Those from other countries, though, have the right to put their names, addresses, and photographs in an envelope and send it to a specific post office box. For more information, visit www.travel.state.gov; click on the hyperlink for Diversity Visa [Year] Instructions.

"Ten to 14 million apply each year for the green card lottery, which sounds like a lot," Yale-Loehr says. However, the odds of getting selected are much greater than winning any state lottery, so it could well pay to keep trying the lottery year after year.

Only one application per year is permitted for the green card lottery, Yale-Loehr advises. "If they catch you sending in more than one, they will disqualify you."

"There are a few things you can do to increase your chances of winning the Green Card lottery," suggests J. Stephen Wilson, co-author of *Win the Green Card Lottery* (Self-Counsel Press, 2002). For one thing, if your spouse applies separately, you can double your chances of winning, he says. Also, if you have the option, charge the registration to a low-admission country. Information on low-admission countries is published by the state department in July for the previous year's diversity visa lottery. If you happen to win this lottery, be sure to send in your forms immediately, Wilson warns. Only half of those initially selected receive a card.

Obtaining an Employment Green Card

If you're looking to work in the United States, it's not enough just to get an employer to sponsor you for a green card. Most employment green card categories also require an employer to advertise and prove to the satisfaction of the U.S. Labor Department that there are no U.S. workers who can do the job. "That can be quite difficult," Yale-Loehr says. "It's not like you can walk in and say, 'I'm here and ready to work and be able to get a green card that way. Moreover, because of the backlogs by the U.S. immigration service, it can take three to four years to get a green card."

Thus, he suggests, it could prove easier to first enter the United States on a temporary visa. Categories of temporary visas include student, tourist, or temporary work visas.

"Some of the categories for (a temporary) work (visa) are not that difficult to obtain," Yale-Loehr says. The most common category is an H-1B temporary work visa. Requirements for an H-1B include these:

- An applicant must have a Bachelor's degree.
- The employer must be hiring the person for a job that requires a Bachelor's degree. "You can't have someone with a Bachelor's degree working at McDonalds or some one with a Bachelor's degree in physics going to teach French," he stresses.
- You must be paid the prevailing wage so that you're not displacing U.S. workers.

Unlike a permanent work visa, the H-1B temporary visa has no employer labor test. It is effective up to six years. During that period, Yale-Loehr suggests, an employer may be able to go through the required process to get you a permanent visa.

Don't have a Bachelor's degree? Then your options for obtaining a temporary work visa in the United States are much more limited. "There's an H-2B category, but it requires a labor market test—just like the one for a green card," Yale-Loehr says. "It also requires that the job duration be less than one year." So, the H-2B may work for persons working in jobs such as a summer camp counselor or a chef at a resort.

Getting a Family Member to Sponsor You

Do you have a family member who can sponsor you for a visa? If so, it's best if you happen to be the spouse of a U.S. citizen, parent of a U.S. citizen, or child of a U.S. citizen under the age of 21, Yale-Loehr says. That's because if you fit into one of those relationships, there is no waiting period to immigrate to the United States. If your child already is a U.S. citizen, he or she must be at least 21 years-old to sponsor you in this category.

Don't fit into any of the above immediate family relationships? Expect a long wait, Yale-Loehr says, based upon which of the following "family preference" sponsorship categories you do fit into.

- "First Preference:" You are an unmarried adult son or daughter of a U.S. citizen and at least 21 years old. Only 23,400 persons in this category may immigrate annually.
- "Second Preference:" You are a spouse, child under 21, or unmarried son or daughter of a permanent resident or green cardholder. Just 114,200 may immigrate annually from this category.
- "Third Preference:" You are a married son or daughter of a U.S. citizen. Just 23,400 in this category can get green cards annually.
- "Fourth Preference:" You are a brother or sister of an adult U.S. citizen. Just 65,000 persons annually may immigrate from this category.

Under a family sponsorship, "only these categories can get green cards," Yale-Loehr says. "If I have an aunt or uncle who is a U.S. citizen, I can't get a green card through them."

"Because of the annual limits (for family sponsorship preference categories), there are backlogs," he adds. In June 2003, for example, there was a 12-year backlog for the Fourth Preference category, which includes brothers and sisters. "That means if I were a U.S. citizen and wanted to file a green card petition for my brother in Mexico, I could file tomorrow, but because of the backlog, it would take 12 years."

So how can you get around the waits? Marriage to a U.S. citizen is one obvious solution, he says. This puts you into the immediate relative category. "The problem is a lot of people commit marriage fraud." As a result, when you marry a U.S. citizen, you get a conditional green card for just two years. "You have to go back to the immigration service and show you're still married," Yale-Loehr says. If you did get divorced and it's not for valid reasons, you probably will lose your green card.

The only other way to cut your waiting time: Have a qualifying relative become a naturalized U.S. citizen.

For example, if someone is married to a green cardholder, normally he or she would have to wait five years in the family sponsored second preference category. "However, once the green cardholder goes through the naturalization process, the spouse gets upgraded to become an immediate relative. So there's no longer a backlog."

Immigration to the United States today is not only tough for those seeking to immigrate. Employers also find themselves at greater risk if they attempt to hire an immigrant with no green card. In 1986, Yale-Loehr notes, Congress passed a law that set up an employer sanctions program. "Now an employer who hires someone without proper papers can be fined. It makes it more difficult for employers who want to obey the law, as well as individuals who want to work but don't have working papers." Yet, he admits, many employers ignore the law.

At last count, there were an estimated 8 million to 12 millions illegal immigrants in the United States, he says. This can create a stressful situation and put illegal immigrants between a rock and a hard place. It's true that the average Mexican worker working here illegally is unlikely to get picked up by the (Bureau of Citizenship and Immigration Services) because that department's resources are limited, he says. Officials are much more concerned right now with finding criminals. On the other hand, illegal immigrants also are unable to get a green card.

This situation, he notes, can trigger a great deal of uncertainty and worry over what will happen if they do get caught. And that can happen. "Maybe they're working in a non-unionized plant, and somebody decides to unionize," he says. If somebody doesn't like that idea, they easily can get rid of all undocumented workers." Or, if someone gets stopped at a traffic light and a police officer asks to see papers, there could be trouble.

But, Yale-Loehr says, the power of the dollar is such that many are willing to take that chance. For more information on visas, visit www.immigration.gov.

Finding a Good Employer

One of the keys to Alex's successful retirement was finding employment with a good organization—one that has attractive employee benefits. It's worth it to inquire about retirement and other job benefits before agreeing to accept a job.

In fact, it might not hurt to tailor your job search to employers that offer attractive benefits. Where should you start? For one thing, attractive benefits often are a cornerstone of jobs offered by U.S. government, state government, and local government agencies.

If that doesn't excite you, you might consider the 10 top-rated companies by The Principal Financial Group in Des Moines, Iowa. The Principal selected these companies as the 10 best companies in the United States out of the 1,000 that it examined in 2003. The insurance company claims that these companies offer strong core benefits, a breadth of benefits that cover all life events; variety, flexibility, help for employees to get the most from their benefits through ongoing education, protection from catastrophic events, and a high commitment to their benefits:

- CEF Industries, Addison, Illinois.
- Delta Dental Plan of Iowa, Ankeny, Iowa.
- Farmers Mutual Hail Insurance Company of Iowa, Des Moines.
- Hypertherm Inc., Hanover, New Hampshire.
- Lancet Software Development Inc., Eagan, Minnesota.
- MEEMIC Insurance Company, Auburn Hills Michigan.
- MSU Federal Credit Union, East Lansing, Michigan.
- Noesis Inc., Manassas, Virginia.
- Parr Instrument Company, Moline, Illinois.
- Strata Environmental Services Inc., Knoxville, Tennessee.

Here are the 20 best large companies to work for in the United States, based on employee benefits, according to *Money* magazine:

- Philip Morris
- Schering-Plough
- K Abbott Laboratories
- TIAA-CREF
- Anheuser-Busch
- Pharmacia
- Anadarko Petroleum
- Northwestern Mutual » Merck
- Eli Lilly
- American Airlines
- Avista Corp.
- Bristol-Myers-Squibb
- Procter & Gamble

- Guardian Life
- United Parcel Service
- Caterpillar
- Freddie Mac
- Allstate
- American Express

Source: *Money* ©2002 Time Inc. All Rights Reserved.

This 2002 list was based upon a poll of Fortune 300 companies in which more than one third responded. The evaluation is based on benefits awarded to a married 50-year-old with two dependent children and 10 years of service who is earning $100,000 a year.

Chapter 9

Larry and Kris Ferstenou: Planning Early Did the Trick

Financial planners have been telling us for years that the younger you are when you start planning for your retirement, the more money you'll have and the earlier you can retire. Larry and Kris Ferstenou actually followed this advice. They started planning for retirement in their mid-20s. And the result was that they were able to retire in their 40s with $500,000.

The couple reached their objective of having enough money to retire in 1993. When we talked with them, they had been retired a decade. Larry, 52, had his own business as a vocational evaluator before he retired at age 42. Kris, 50, worked as a school teacher and subsequently launched her own business in accounting before retiring at age 40. Between the two, they averaged $48,000 annually over their working life—capping out at nearly $100,000 annually in three years before they wound down their work lives. Neither had a pension. Neither collects Social Security.

Haifa million dollars might sound like a lot, but at today's low interest rates, it doesn't generate as much income as you'd think. The main reason is because people who retire in their 40s will likely live well into their 80s. As a result, their money has to last. Over the long term prices will rise, so a retiree's nest egg also must grow to keep pace with inflation.

Larry and Kris love to talk about their accomplishment of retiring early. Imagine: no work, no bosses, no meetings, no office politics, and no fighting traffic to get to and from work. "Most people could do this if they wanted to," Larry says. "Those who are motivated, who apply good discipline to savings. They can retire young."

At this writing, the Ferstenous live comfortably in a 1,500-square-foot townhouse in a planned 92-unit community on the red terrain of Ivins, Utah, a bedroom community of St. George. Their home has two bedrooms, two baths, and an office. To the rear of their home is Red Mountain, and they are near Snow Canyon State Park. Their community has an exercise room and swimming pools. Initially, they rented in a 16-unit attached townhouse complex in the area. Although they were able to walk everywhere, they decided that they wanted more amenities. So they moved to a detached townhouse complex outside the main activity of the city. That's where they decided to buy. Their current development largely is comprised of retirees.

It's true the couple makes some trade-offs for their lifestyle. For example, they don't travel much. "If Kris and I wanted to travel to Australia and Europe once a year, it would be pretty hard to do on our budget," Larry admits. "Your friends are all working," Kris adds. "You can see them only on evenings and weekends."

They also have not given up work entirely. But unlike the majority of working stiffs, the little work they do is only what they choose to do. They do it strictly on their own terms and have specific criteria for the work they will accept. Larry typically busies himself with odd jobs—often painting or maintenance work a few days a month for friends. He does only work that allows him flexibility and is totally different from the work he did in his career. However, when we talked with him, he was even doing very little of that. He had been writing his book, *You Can Retire Young* (American Book Business Press, 2002).

Larry and Kris worked together to make their dream of early retirement come true. As their incomes grew, the two avoided succumbing to traps that many fall into. For example, the home they bought in 1986 was smaller and less expensive than they could have bought. They both made what some might consider to be sacrifices, which can be tough to do when you are young and want to enjoy life.

Perhaps one reason this couple succeeded in reaching their goal of early retirement while many others would consider it a pipe dream is that the couple suffered a major tragedy in their lives. Larry's father died of a fatal heart attack in 1977 at the age of 52. Larry was 26. "That had a major impact on Kris and me," Larry says. "We were young, starting our careers. We had been married one year. We decided we didn't want to work until we died."

When the couple first married in Wisconsin, they had $5,000 in savings and $11,000 in student loan debt. Kris had most of the debt. They were undeterred. "We knew the only way we'd go through college is by working and having debt," she says. Fortunately, her teaching loans were at low interest rates—about 3 percent. She also was able to get a break on some of that interest in exchange for agreeing to work with lower-income school districts. Larry's loans, accruing at least 6 percent interest, were the priority. "We paid those off immediately in the first three years of being married," he says.

By the end of their first year of marriage, they already had begun tracking income and expenses. After they were married 10 years, they had saved $97,000, which they kept largely in savings accounts and CDs. During the second 10 years of their marriage, as their income grew, they amassed more than $500,000. They did this largely by funding tax-advantaged retirement plans to the maximum.

Originally, the couple had aimed to retire when Larry was 50 with at least $1 million. But when Larry was 42, they decided that with some $500,000, they already had enough to take the plunge. "If we were to continue working, we would have had more money, but that wasn't enough of an attraction," Larry says.

Larry had been managing five employees and was suffering the stress of dealing with injured workers, the state of California, and insurance companies. "We were working seven days a week with businesses," Kris explains. "We needed to spend more time with each other and with family and friends. We tried to scale back, but a business is pretty hard to scale back."

Over the years, the couple invested wisely and their wealth grew. When we first talked to them, their net worth hovered around $750,000, thanks to the bull market of the 1990s. They managed to preserve their net worth throughout that difficult bear market period of March 2000 into 2003, largely, they believe, because they had more free time to monitor the market. Of course, the couple also has no children.

In the late 1990s, Larry began spending much of his leisure time looking at the history of the stock market. "Frankly, we started getting a little scared that we were going to take a major dive," he says. "We saw what has happened. The market was doing 20 percent and we knew bear markets happen every five years on average."

In 1998 and 1999, he started selling his riskier growth stock funds and moving into lower-risk bonds and real estate investment trusts (REITs). Then the bear market hit and stocks took a nosedive. Yet, Larry figures that the couple's holdings were down just about 8.2 percent at the end of December 2002 versus at the end of December 1999. Not bad, considering that the S&P 500 index, a measure of stock market performance, fell some 43 percent during that period. His bonds and REITs, he says, were doing well.

Larry said he enjoys going to the library and reading as much as he can. Had he been working, Larry figures, the declining stock market might have proven much more painful because he would not have had time to devote to his investments and make the necessary changes.

Today, Larry feels little obligation to make enough to contribute to his retirement.

Kris does, however. "He made more money," Kris explains. He had the opportunity to do a 403 (b) retirement plan and got started much earlier." Kris admits that even in retirement, she has found a need to draw the line on work. In 1997 and she was helping a company open another corporation— a job that took a good chunk of her time. Then the company opened yet another corporation in Nevada. "In the summer of we came back from a trip we had made. They decided they were going to open two more companies," she says. "When I got back and saw the increased workload, I resigned the same day."

The couple says they had been starting to lose track of why they had retired. Since then, she has been doing much less work. The ideal early retirement work, Larry says, is doing odd projects that last just three to five days. Their goal is merely to pick up enough income to fund their retirement plans.

In 2002, Kris made $10,000 and put $7,500 of that into a SIMPLE (Savings Incentive Match Plan for Employees) plan. Under this retirement plan, for employers with 100 or fewer employees, contributions are typically not taxed until they are withdrawn. For 2003, she had planned to cut back her workload, doing closer to $6,000 worth of business. She was considering opening a spousal IRA for Larry under her business.

"I had a SEP (Simplified Employee Pension) plan in California," Kris says. "However, the newer SIMPLE plan is easier to administer and handle." She can shelter every penny she earns. A SEP, she explains, is more limited as to how much she can put in.

The two say that in 2002, they actually budgeted $1,600. Altogether, they spent just $1,324 monthly, or $15,888 plus another $300 per month in mad money from their part-time jobs. "That included my expenses for back surgery," Kris says, noting that the actual expenditures included an out-of-the-ordinary $2,500 for her insurance deductible.

It's true that health insurance could pose a serious concern down the road, they say. Its cost is going through the roof. They use Regence Blue Cross/Blue Shield of Utah, a preferred provider network (PPN).

Maintaining control over health insurance costs, they acknowledge, is a constant battle. Upon moving to Utah from California, they were able to slice their health insurance at least in half to $135 monthly because health insurance costs vary by geographic area. However, when the premium was to rise from $135 to $210 monthly, they increased their deductible to $2,500, bringing the price down to $175. Around 1999, the couple made yet another change. They found that by reapplying to the same insurance company, they were able to lower their rate from $175 monthly to $135 monthly. The insurance company evidently had price incentives for new customers. They were careful to hold on to their old policies until they were accepted as new customers, to make certain their coverage did not lapse.

The Ferstenous stress, though, that not everybody is in a position to reapply for health insurance. Not all insurance companies may operate the same way. Also, if you cancel the insurance policy and have health problems, you may have difficulty getting new insurance. In 2003, their premiums were $185.

Although they continue to have a small life insurance policy that Kris had through her credit union, they generally avoid carrying any more life insurance. It is one of the most expensive financial services, and both figure that if something happens to one of them, they will have enough to take care of themselves. Plus, both are still capable of working. "We never thought we needed to make money off the other's death," Larry says.

The Ferstenous are careful shoppers. They have to make their money last, so they pay close attention to what they buy. They avoid impulse buying; instead, they look for the best quality at the best price. For example, a reliable car is one of the most important purchases a retiree can make. It may cost a little more to purchase a car that lasts, but it is worth it. The ongoing cost of repair can really take a bite out of people's pocketbooks.

When we talked with them, they had one car, a 1997 Honda CR-V sport utility vehicle, which had just 48,000 miles. They had driven a 1980 Plymouth Champ until their 1993 retirement and had driven their 1984 Toyota Camry until they sold it in 1999. They refrained from buying fancy cars and claim they have owned only four vehicles.

They don't mind paying more for major purchases in exchange for good quality. Kris and Larry carefully evaluate each purchase, and major purchases always are discussed with one another. Fortunately, the two are similar in their spending habits. Kris says she gets her thriftiness from her father, who never buys anything unless he has cash to pay. "We've always agreed on everything we bought that costs any money," Larry adds.

Of course there are little spats. "I just bought a new refrigerator and we didn't need a new one," Kris acknowledged. Larry was not thrilled with the purchase. But Kris figured she had back surgery and wanted a refrigerator designed so that she didn't have to bend so much. Larry finally agreed.

"When we got married, my mother said to buy good bedroom furniture," Kris says. "We bought solid oak. It still looks brand new." She bought a reliable Maytag washer and dryer that she says has held up for 26 years. Only recently did she buy a new set that included a front-loader washing machine, which is believed to be more water- and energy-efficient.

They also are not afraid to buy used items. "We had a friend who had to have a new big-screen TV," Larry said. As a result, the couple was able to get his slightly used 26-inch television for a song. So far, they have had it five years. They also shop for clearance merchandise. The two say they shop at Costco, buying in bulk at lower cost. They try to go to the last matinee at movie theaters, to take advantage of discounted prices, and they use food coupons and frequent early bird specials at restaurants. "We've been married 26 years," Kris said. "We've built five new homes.

We've always had a new home, new car, and nice furniture in the home. What we try to save on are all the little things people don't think of—like eating out." Their freezer is always full, she adds, because they buy meat when it goes on sale.

Both try to stay in good health, getting in at least two hours of physical activity daily. They admit they have some fears now that they've retired early of taking care of their aging parents. Their parents have no long-term care insurance.

Right now, Kris says, her parents and Larry's mother are very healthy. "So we try not to worry about it." They've thought that if anything happened, they might buy a piece of property large enough to lodge both families. "We can see where our budget can very possibly change," Larry says. "Right now, we live cheaply, compared with most people."

If you are the type of person who wants to retire early, one of the most important things you can do is lower your cost of living. In his book, Larry suggests that you compare quarterly cost-of-living indexes issued by The American Chamber of Commerce Researchers Association (ACCRA), at www.accra.org. The average is 100. St. George falls fairly close to average.

Before the couple moved from California to the St. George area, they had determined the type of location they wanted. Their goal was to find a city of less than 50,000 people that was clean and that had low crime and no snow. They wanted a good public library, discount movie theaters, bowling, tennis, hiking, cultural activities, and beautiful scenery. They also aimed to be relatively close to a large city. They clearly have reached their goal.

Today the Ferstenous calculate their net worth every three months, adding up all their assets so they know where they stand. They have no debt. Originally, they started investing with a stockbroker because they say they had no clue about what they were doing with their money. Subsequently, they switched largely to no-load mutual funds. "I don't recommend a broker necessarily for people unless they don't want to do it on their own," Larry says.

Doing It Yourself

Want to retire young like Larry and Kris? You can retire early if you make up your mind to do so. Of course, it takes a lot of cooperation from family members.

"One huge mistake people make is they spend an inordinate amount of time figuring how much money they're going to need," says retirement planning expert John F. Wasik, author of *Retire Early—and Live, the Life You Want Now* (Henry Holt, 2001). Add up the figures, he says, and it may seem useless. But, Wasik says, "you can make one or two decisions to make it affordable at an earlier age."

One example, Wasik says, might be simply to relocate your home. "If you're living in a very expensive metropolitan area and you decide to move to Vero Beach, Florida, you can take $300,000 from the sale of your home and buy a nice condo for $150,000." If you're married and filing a joint return, you needn't pay capital gains tax on up to $500,000 of profit on your home—provided that you and your spouse have lived in the home for two of the previous five years. You might invest that profit and use it to help jump-start your retirement, he says.

You also need to determine the lifestyle you would like when you retire. "Some retirees when they get out of the work force don't know what to do with themselves," he says. "Consider the intellectual, creative, spiritual, and social aspects of your nature."

Once you've decided how you'd like to spend your retired life, you can nail down your goals and determine how they relate to what you're spending money on. Then figure out how much more you'll need to save to accomplish your goals.

The earlier you start this exercise, the better. Wasik suggests you tally up all your assets. For each investment, figure out how much you expect it to give you in monthly income when you retire. How much do you think you'll be getting from stock and bond dividends and interest? How much from real estate rental income? How much from retirement plans? Add in any income you anticipate from part-time work that you expect to continue once you retire. Then add all your monthly income streams and multiply the total by 4 to 6 percent to determine the most you'd likely withdraw on a monthly basis. The lower factor is more apt to give you income for a longer period.

You also have to consider how long your money will last. At today's low interest rates, your money can still last a long time. For example, if you withdraw 4 percent of your money each year and your investment earns 4 percent, the money will last indefinitely. Even if you withdraw 4 percent and your investment grows 3 percent, the money will last 45 years. Say you withdraw 6 percent out of your investments each year: If the investment earns 5 percent, the money would last 34 years. Assume that the stock market performs well and interest rates are higher: If you withdrew 8 percent and your investment grows 7 percent, your money would last 27 years.

Next, list all your monthly expenses—including health-care premiums, loans, mortgages, and daily entertainment. Don't forget medical expenses and discretionary spending. Do you plan to buy a second home? Do you need to help your children and grandchildren financially?

Don't worry if the picture looks dim. You have Social Security benefits, and you might not need as much. Also, even if you don't take off for a lower-cost condo in sunny climates, maybe your home will be paid off.

To get the projected monthly stream more in line with your expenses, go through each expenses and determine whether they might be cut.

Inflation will play a large part in estimating your family's future income and expenses. If you tie up all your money in bonds and CDs, you may lose purchasing power because your income stays the same, while your costs are rising.

Investments that have historically appreciated in value more than inflation include stocks and real estate. Stocks have grown at almost 8 percent annually after inflation over the past seven decades, according to Ibbotson Associates in Chicago. Real estate has typically grown at 3 percent more than inflation.

One rule of thumb is that you should plan to draw about 70 to 80 percent of your current income from your retirement savings in addition to Social Security. Based on this, if you make $70,000 a year, you will need a retirement kitty of $523,000 to provide you with a target annual income of about $53,000.

Again, this calculation figures that your money grows at 8 percent annually and that you retire at age 67 to qualify for Social Security.

Historically, a mix of 60 percent stocks and 40 percent bonds has grown at an annual rate of more than 8 percent since 1926. So the younger you are, the less you have to invest each month to reach your goal. Can't quite swing early retirement yet?

Open up both a Roth IRA and a SEP-IRA or SIMPLE plan if you qualify, or consider fully funding your tax-deferred IRA. You still have until April 15 of each year to make your contribution. Take it from the Ferstenous: The power of tax deferral can dramatically accelerate your efforts.

Chapter 10

Dennis Hastings: Native American Anthropologist Beating Stroke

Dennis Hastings, 54, might seem to have the toughest retirement story of anyone in this book. A Native American, he overcame abandonment as a child and a grueling life at Indian boarding schools to finally accomplish something almost unheard of for a person of his background. He obtained a Master's degree in anthropology at the Western Institute for Social Research. As his Master's thesis, he co-authored a book with Robin Ridington, *Blessings for a Long Time* (University of Nebraska Press, 1997). Unfortunately, almost immediately after these accomplishments, Dennis was cruelly forced into retirement by a severe stroke in the prime of his life.

But that doesn't stop him from continuing to lead a fulfilling and meaningful life. Dennis has found a way to live comfortably and continue in anthropology. Today the divorced father of three lives alone in a double-wide prefab home in Waltham, Nebraska. He is on the reservation of his native Indian tribe, the Omahas, on the Missouri River. His annual income is down from a peak of $27,000 annually to some $500 monthly of Social Security disability income.

As founder and director of a nonprofit 501 (c) corporation, the Omaha Tribal Historical Research Project (OTHRP), he is attempting to raise money to build a landmark museum for his tribe. "I can't just sit there like a bump on a log," he says.

Dennis grew up largely in the care of a great-grandmother, Mary Burt Hastings. He was ordered surrendered when his great-grandmother became too old to take care of him at the age of 6. "I found out they took her to an old folk's home." He doesn't like to talk about his father, who, as an adult, later sent for him and served as a positive, hard-working role model. His mother died when he was young. He also doesn't like to talk about his five-year-long marriage, which ended in divorce.

He lived his childhood mostly at the Wahpeton Indian School in North Dakota. In those days, orphaned Native Americans were placed in government or religious schools. Today Dennis is still surprised at how far away from his family he was ordered sent: The school was more than 300 miles away. "It wasn't very loving," he says. "First of all, when they put tribes together not knowing each other, it can be pretty devastating. You've got to remember these are tribal people that fought a long time ago. Now they're being put together."

Dennis says his hair was cut above his ears. Beatings at Indian schools were said to be frequent. Educators suppressed tribal languages and cultural practices. Children were taught manual labor. "We lined up," he reflects. "They said, 'What religion do you belong to?' I said, 'I don't know.' They counted some out and said, 'You're going to be Episcopalian.' To me and four other guys: 'You're going to be a Catholic.'"

Dennis says he remembers that while normal school dormitories today are shared by two persons in a room, the boarding school dormitories had 80 to 150 children sleeping in bunk beds in one room. Teachers made the children line up and march in the dinner line. Matrons forced them to line up in their dormitory area. Often Dennis worried about the condition of his great-grandmother, but he had no money to call her. "I would go to people to see if they could call down there," he says. The insensitive response: 'No. They don't have the budget.'"

Fights in line were a way of life. Once Dennis actually was punched by a Chippewa Indian who worked at the school. As Dennis tried to escape, his fist smashed through the window and he had to have several stitches.

He remembers lining up in the "west basement" and being ordered to sit down and keep quiet. One of the matrons charged that somebody did something. "My name was involved," he recalls. "I stood up and said 'No, I didn't.'" They just picked rne out and started to punish me. I found out later on that punishment can mean anything. The whole school was trying to belittle you. They were trying to carry on an agenda to keep Indians down."

Dennis said the attitudes about Indians stemmed from people in the town in which employees lived.

Often he felt like running away. In fact, he says, he did—70-something times. Unfortunately, though, school was the only home he had, so he had no choice but to return.

Dennis always felt bitter inside about his situation at school. "I felt it was tearing down my inner emotions," he says. However, one teacher interested him in classical music and art. Dennis found that he enjoyed reading and often went to the library. Although reading initially was a struggle, he got people to read to him. In the library, he found a book by Francis LaFlesche, a noted anthropologist. Dennis was amazed to learn that LaFlesche actually was an Indian from the Omaha Nation—just like him. He became especially curious to learn how this Indian had survived such a difficult existence and read everything he could about him.

It was common for Indians in boarding schools to be told they would never amount to anything. When it's said enough times, you often believe it's true. However, Dennis said that an inner voice told him to fight back. "If you look at my school record, I always was in trouble because I fought back," he says. Although he was told that he would get into trouble if he kept it up, fighting back may well have been the only thing that kept him alive.

He went on to attend Flandreau Indian School, another boarding school, in South Dakota. There, he says, he realized that although he might not like the situation, he had the power to educate himself and better himself. "They didn't talk to us about universities—not very much." He says about five times a year, he was ready to give up. "I would go deep into myself for two or three days and have a mind change." Throughout his school years, he worked—not for money, but for room and board. Once he had to get up at 5 A.M. to work in a bakery. "I thought it was fun," he says. "That woman who worked in the bakery was German—a big lady. She was nice. She would bake bread and would always let us have something."

After high school, Dennis signed up to go to another Indian school in Kansas but then decided against it. "I was tired of government schools. I just wandered around for a few years here and there, doing farm work—anything I could get my hands on. I cut meat at an Iowa beef plant. You got a good salary—$3-something an hour.

Dennis also served in Vietnam, but he prefers not to discuss that. "I wish I went to Canada," he says in retrospect. Finally, his father, who had been living in California, found him. "I was at the point where I needed to go out and visit him for the pure wonderment of what he is and what he looks like." Dennis says he spent his own money to fly to Sacramento to see his dad. "After being separated from him and all that, I came to the realization that he always did think of me."

His father worked for the Southern Pacific Railroad. I went out there, stayed with him, and worked there. He encouraged me to be a good man." Dennis says he found it interesting to see his father working every day. He noted that his grandfather also worked hard a good part of his life. 'The male people in my family were good workers," he says. At one point, Dennis heard news on the radio about Indians taking over Alcatraz Island and decided to see what was happening.

That's when Dennis started getting involved in Indian rights activities. He helped in the 19-month takeover of Alcatraz Island. In 1973, he organized the shipment of food and supplies to Indians when the American Indian Movement took over Wounded Knee in South Dakota. "We got clothing, food, and all that stuff and went in a caravan," he said. "I can't remember how many cars we had." Two people were reported killed during the 71-day occupation.

Dennis often was outspoken in favor of Indian rights and was instrumental in negotiating the return of Indian artifacts to the Omaha tribe. In fact, Dennis helped spearhead repatriation legislation in Nebraska that allowed the tribe to obtain skeletal remains that had been taken by the state. After his effort, a federal repatriation law also was adopted.

Dennis had earned a Bachelor's degree from the New School of California in 1984.

He initially supported himself by working in social services for the state of California, earning about $27,000 annually. However, he frequently kept in touch with relatives on his reservation. A call finally came asking if he could return and work for the tribe. "I said, 'Well, I've got to think about it.'"

Although Dennis finally was starting to get ahead financially, it was important for him to revisit the youth that he had missed.

"I got in my Jeep and loaded it up and told the place I worked to give me a year's leave of absence. They approved it. I never did go back."

Initially, his job with the Omaha Nation forced him to take a pay cut. In fact, his pay was sporadic, at best, largely dependent upon what type of grants he was able to obtain. Generally, he earned no more than $13,000 or $14,000 annually. Nevertheless, he had wanted to see where his great-grandmother lived and walk the steps she did before she died. At first, he lived in a trailer.

"When it was finally the day to leave and get away, it wasn't a reality," he says. "I knew this is where I was going to live and die."

From that point on, Dennis devoted himself to trying to rebuild the dignity that had been taken away from the Omaha Nation, says Wynema Morris, a staff researcher and tribal member. Morris says that the Omahas proved instrumental in the U.S. victory against the British in the War of 1812. The Omahas threw their force behind the Americans to help push back the British. Yet people never read about it in the history books.

"He feels as I do, that the Omahas have been overlooked far too much, yet they were such a great power," she says. The Omahas once controlled land that extended east of the Mississippi River. Now they are relegated to 14 square miles of land around the Missouri River. Many are losing their culture and are leaving the area. Eighty to 85 percent are unemployed.

Dennis continued to be outspoken in Indian causes. In 1992, he obtained press coverage for his criticism of Gen. Lee Butler, in the aftermath of the Persian Gulf War. In a toast to Vice President Dick Cheney—then Secretary of Defense— Butler claimed that the U.S. military had put Iraqi president Saddam Hussein "back on the reservation."

Dennis took widely publicized offense. "I expected a little more dignity to our people," Dennis retorted. Butler quickly apologized.

***

Dennis finally earned his Master's degree in anthropology in May, 1998. He had received a scholarship from the American Association for Community Based Education to continue his education at Western Institute for Social Research (WISR). WISR is a small, nontraditional Berkeley, California institution that encourages students to study in their own communities and is dedicated to peaceful and constructive social change. But immediately after he realized his dream to obtain the degree, he was fallen by a stroke. Dennis doesn't like to talk much about that bleak period of his life.

"Your mouth is going in the opposite direction," he says. "It was very devastating for me at that period of time. I tried so hard to get a Master's degree. I slid right underneath the carpet and couldn't get out. I can't think very good. My language is not very good. It's going to be permanent." Even today he gets confused when he tries to remember dates or other numbers.

Despite his latest round of misfortune, Dennis's personal debt situation wasn't too bad then. He was doing something he loved. His burning desire still is to get the museum built.

Today Dennis continues to do what he loves, but he lives on less. He lives frugally in a mobile home. He avoids debt and gets free medical care on the reservation.

"My biggest debt right now is the trailer," he says. "It's already half paid for." He says he bought the trailer for about $65,000 three years ago and financed it with a Veterans Administration loan. "I have a little 1989 Ford Probe. It just got hit by a deer the other night. I felt bad for the deer and I felt bad for the car." The car was out of commission when we first talked with him.

Yet somehow, Morris observes, Dennis always manages to have a set of wheels. "He's an excellent mechanic," Morris explains. It is not uncommon, she says, for people to give him an old car that no longer works. Or, he will buy a very cheap car that's virtually worthless. Generally, the cars he buys have more than 100,000 miles. "Dennis will take that car and get it running. I've seen him in one year have three or four different cars and get them running."

If Dennis happens to be without wheels, he typically won't ask for a ride. His feeling about cars, she says: "If it goes out on me, it means that car's never going to run again."

Morris notes that he has two computers that have been donated to him on behalf of the OTHRP. "Actually, I think he's had three. I think that one just gave out altogether." Friends often help. Morris admits that if she felt Dennis couldn't do something, she would take him a bag of groceries or sometimes have him come over and eat. "It's not that often because I don't want to wound his pride, but he manages to eat well enough." Fortunately for Dennis, she says, he lives in farm country, where fruits and vegetables are cheap and plentiful.

Hastings says that his modest home sits on some 80 acres that he inherited from his grandfather. But he shares the land with other heirs, and the land technically is held in trust by the U.S. government. As a result, Dennis can't sell it. Instead, he gets about $200 annually for rent collected by the U.S. government, which leases it to farmers. This is one of the many ways that Native Americans have been given a raw deal, he says.

Despite his tight existence, money never was a concern in Dennis's life. "I don't know if it was the situation I was in— they never allowed me to think that way. Sure enough, I like nice things. I just never had the background. I'm not foolish with money. I'm very frugal." Morris notes that Dennis's home is decorated very tastefully, with artist sketches of Indian women. He also has an attractive kitchen set.

"(My income) doesn't meet expenses, but I keep doing things. Eventually something happens. Say I needed a car payment. I don't buy lavish cars. I do a contract and wait for that money to get here and pay it off. The creditors are very mad at me. By the time the year's ended, they're not so mad.

"There's no personal debt like I used to have. There's some organizational debt. Various board members and people are helping me now because I've worked on this museum for a good many years. We've got to the point where we can show it now. We have an architect on board My goal now is to see our museum finished. It's going to be right on the river. The tribe donated 1,600 acres of land to us so we can build it."

Dennis says that the reservation today has younger people. The older people are dying off.

Dennis gets no salary for his efforts to get his tribe's museum off the ground. At this writing, he estimates that the organization is $300 to $400 in the red. That's not uncommon. Frequently, notes Morris, the very committed board of directors helps out personally with the situation. But despite the lack of any funding, Dennis already is pretty far along with his plans.

Architect Vincent Snyder, a native of Wahoo, Nebraska, now in Austin, Texas, designed a 45,000-square-foot museum to be built on a bluff 270 feet above the flood plain overlooking the Missouri River. "I used to go to pow-wows when I was in seventh and eighth grade and was actually in boxing tournaments," says Snyder, who won several awards for the pro bono design. "It just seemed like it would be a real shame. It's such an important project, they deserved really the best building they could get." The cultural interpretive center will lodge more than 1,300 of the tribe's cultural items and documents. It also will contain classrooms, a research library, a conference room, a gift shop, a restaurant, and an office.

Among the artifacts it is expected to lodge is a coveted sacred pole, which Dennis was instrumental in getting returned to Nebraska from the Peabody Museum in Cambridge. The 6-foot-long pole, made of cottonwood, is believed to be 400 years old and to hold the powers to guide, unify, and renew.

He is working on trying to get some grants for his project, but he says that money in this economy has dried up.

Dennis says that his creed has been to deal with his situation the best that he can. "Keep your head above water, and smile and laugh as much as you can about life." He also is putting his resources into his museum. "What I mean about a museum is, it will be part museum, but with other things in there. I call it an interpretive center, a place where culture is going to be. It's a place where poor kids can go and look at movies about their culture. They can look at the whole river and feel proud of themselves and the land around them. When your whole world has been turned upside down and it's ruined, how can you take it? How can you take it and make it better?"

Dennis says that if he had such a museum when he was growing up, it would have put him "on a real positive axis. You've got to remember that our culture tried to help the white race accomplish what they were trying to do. We made every treaty with the U.S. government. They still chose to oppress us. It was a real big blow to us.

"I'm doing the best I can."

The stroke has distracted Dennis from any desire to save money and get ahead, but his mind-set right now is getting the museum built for the tribe so that their lives can be better. "I see a lot of these poor kids walking around, and I say, 'Wouldn't it be nice to have a museum that's really completed?' They could say, 'This is all mine, and I didn't have to pay for it.'"

In fact, he says, his positive attitude largely has fueled his existence. He does his therapy exercises in the morning. Occasionally, he gets up to go to a movie. "I just go by myself," he says. "My imagination is not dead."

In some ways, he believes, he is luckier than some wealthier people who have gotten laid off from jobs in major cities. There is a unique camaraderie among Indians. In the large cities, he says, "if you lose your job, it's very scary. You don't have people to meet the social needs you might have. People are not organized in that way with groups of people to help each other.

"I think some of the churches are probably helping out. The country towns are really something. You can park in the middle of the road in the country and visit for an hour. People are very social."

Each day he tries to go into town, either to Macy or Waltham. He might pick up some pork chops and rice and put it in his refrigerator for a few days. He reads the newspaper. Although he might be entitled to food stamps, he shuns them. "It's got an aura that you're at the last of your hopes and you're down on the ground and out," he says. "I know I'm down there, but I want to believe that I can do something for myself. I try to survive that way."

Dennis expects that his affliction will never let him work again. Nevertheless, his innate positive attitude propels him to continue plugging away at a more important cause.

Doing It Yourself

Sometimes life isn't fair. A stroke cut down Dennis Hastings in the prime of his life. He didn't make a lot of money when he was a working professional, but he loved his job as an anthropologist, an author, and the historian for the Omaha Nation American Indian tribe.

Dennis was hampered right from the start. Although he had the good fortune to inherit an allotment of land, he's limited to what he can do with it. In fact, he told us, in the first two years after he moved there, he actually had to pay rent for his own land!

Chris Stainbrook, president of the nonprofit Indian Land Tenure Foundation in Little Canada, Missouri, says Dennis's land situation is not uncommon among Native Americans.

At fault largely is the General Allotment Act, also known as the Dawes Act of 1887, which authorized the U.S. government to divide reservations and allot tracts of land to individual Indians.

Each Indian head of household got 160 acres, single individuals got 80 acres, children under 18 received 40 acres, and the remaining surplus reservation land was opened to homesteaders.

But although they were allotted land, American Indians were not permitted to write wills until 1910. As a result, the title to each allotment was divided equally among virtually every eligible heir. "Some properties have more than probably 3,000 or 4,000 owners," Stainbrook explains. In fact, even after 1910, many American Indians failed to write wills.

Owners of the allotments often get money from the Bureau of Indian Affairs, which, due to the unwieldy number of owners, wound up administering farm leases on the land. But lease money is divided among so many owners that the amount an individual gets, if any, often is minute.

Stainbrook said that if, like Dennis, you happen to own an allotment that has been passed down to you through the generations, you should follow these tips:

- Consolidate ownership of your land so that you can gain control of enough land to do something with it. This way, you at least stand a chance of building a house on it or developing it. You might consider consolidating the land by trading it, gifting the deed, or buying out the other owners.
- Make sure you have wills that are specific about the disposition of the property. Keep in mind that you may need more than one will, based on the nature of the land that has been passed on to you. You should have separate wills for trust land on a reservation, which is an ownership interest in an allotment; fee land on a reservation, which is land that has been taken out of the trust and is owned by the

individual; and fee land that is off the reservation. Make certain that the wills have broad language to include land that may be in the process of accruing to your estate.
- Immediately understand exactly what land you own. "Sometimes that isn't really apparent," Stainbrook says. "You basically have to push the bureau agency office at each reservation to give you a full accounting of it."

Be aggressive not only in pursuing information, but also in trying to get the consolidation of ownership. For more information, visit www.indianlandtenure.org or contact 651-766-8999 or info@indianlandtenure.org.

Qualifying for Social Security Disability

Fortunately, Dennis qualified for Social Security disability, a program designed to allow people who are unable to work a way to tap their Social Security benefits.

You are eligible for monthly Social Security disability checks, provided that you have worked in jobs that are covered by Social Security. You also must have a medical condition that meets Social Security's definition of disability. If you think you might be eligible for Social Security disability, call 1-800-772-1213 or visit www.ssa.gov.

To determine whether you're disabled, an evaluation is made of the following criteria:
- Are you working? If so, you generally may not be averaging more than $800 monthly in 2003.
- Is your condition severe? Your condition must interfere with basic work-related activities.
- Does your condition appear on a list of disabling medical conditions? If not, is your condition equal in severity to conditions found on this list?
- If it is not as severe as a medical condition on the list, can you do the work you did previously?
- Can you do any other type of work?

No benefits are paid for partial disability or short-term disability. You generally start getting paid for the sixth full month after the date your disability is found to have started.

Stanley F. Denman, a Dallas-based Social Security disability attorney, says that if you expect to collect Social Security disability, you should apply immediately. Often, he says, workers are required to have worked 20 of the last 40 calendar quarters to qualify. Any delays in applying can hurt their chances.

Denman advises that if you want to make sure that you continue to qualify for disability income, you should see your doctor regularly; follow your doctor's advice; take your medication, if prescribed; don't give up; and have some type of plan for how you're going to manage the illness and get beyond it.

"If medicines are prescribed for you, you need to take them," Denman warns. "A fair number of people I see will claim to have excruciating pain and won't take their medicine. They'll say they don't want to get addicted to it." Persons who say they won't take their medicine, he says, are apt to be viewed suspiciously during a review.

Denman warns that the laws governing Social Security disability are extremely convoluted, and it is dangerous to make assumptions. For example, in 2003, you are not disabled if your earnings average more than $800 monthly. However, this doesn't always mean that you can collect disability and still earn $800 monthly.

"The government can do what's called a disability review of somebody at any point in time," he says. "They can review you and say, 'Well, I don't think you're disabled any longer.'"

Any earnings showing up for a disabled person, he says, could attract a review.

Keeping a Positive Attitude

If you are disabled or elderly and have no money due to circumstances beyond your control, you can get help. Getting help doesn't make you an unworthy person.

Dr. Viktor Emil Frankl, psychiatrist and author of *Man's Search for Meaning* (Washington Square Press, 1997), suggests that you look adversity squarely in the eyes. Frankel should know. He spent four years in Auschwitz, a Nazi concentration camp. View it as a challenge, he suggests. Also view adversity as giving meaning to your life. You can choose to hang your head and feel helpless, or you can use the experience to spur you on to meaningful activities. In Frankl's case, he found meaning in his life as a concentration camp inmate by trying to help the sick and dying as best as he could. He saw his relationships with people as a blessing.

You must find meaningful things to do with your time. Dennis, for example, still is a tribal historian for the Omaha Nation. He is involved in Indian affairs.

Take your cue from Dennis. Follow your passions. Perhaps you are living on a fixed income and are just getting by.

Get involved in something you enjoy. If you like politics, get involved at the local level with the Democratic, Republican, or Independent political parties.

Get involved with your church, synagogue, mosque, or temple activities.

Do you like to help people? Consider doing some volunteer work at a hospital or nursing home.

Are you an avid sports fan? Look for a club to join. Do you like literature? Write a book. Check out your local public library for reading clubs.

Look for a cause worthy of your time. Get involved. The bottom line: It's your choice.

Chapter 11

Kathleen Maddox: Reversal of Fortune

Kathleen Maddox, 63, of Billings, Montana, is finally starting to enjoy her retirement. She took a trip to visit her sister in Arizona for Thanksgiving in 2002. She was able to spend that Christmas with another sister in Grand Forks, North Dakota. "I think I'm going to join Curves, an exercise program," she says. "I would like to take the boat out of Seattle to Alaska and I have friends up there. That's my next thing."

Kathleen credits a reverse mortgage with changing her life. A reverse mortgage lets you tap the equity in your home for income as long as you live.

Kathleen says she had been lucky most of her life because she didn't have to work—except for a stint as a school lunch aide and some volunteer work. She was a stay-at-home mom of four children who are now all grown. Her husband, Hyman "Carl" Maddox, worked as an engineer for Cenex Pipeline and largely supported the brood. Just when her children were old enough that the couple could enjoy their lives together, both spouses became seriously ill. Suddenly, Kathleen's life took a turn for the worse.

Carl died in 1993 after suffering from non-Hodgkin's lymphoma and prostate cancer. At the same time, Kathleen was stricken with stage-three ovarian cancer. "We cared for each other," she says of that dark period of her life when they both were gravely ill. "Mom came here and lived with us for one year to cook for us. She was 84 at the time and still very able."

Mostly, the couple existed on soup. Although her husband never recovered, Kathleen did. As she attended her husband's funeral, she was in the final stage of her treatment. Ten months later, she was in remission.

It was a difficult time for her. But she persevered because of the people she loved. "It sure lets you know what's important," she says of the ordeal. "But I'm glad I learned what I did. I learned to be strong and patient. I learned that things don't matter. It's your family. It's your friends. How you treat people. That's what's important."

Looking back at her life, she can see how important it is to enjoy life while you are young and healthy, and she urges others to consider that. She suggests that anyone who wants to travel or do anything, "start doing it before you retire." Too often, she says, you hear about people who wanted to do things, and then they lose a spouse or become too ill.

"We had not traveled very much without the children," she says. Most of her recreational life had involved weekend camping trips. She and her husband taught their children to shoot guns safely. "I was brought up in North Dakota, where people were hunters and fisherman," she explains. "My husband enjoyed that. He was from Arkansas originally. He lived in the boonies and shot coon."

The couple bought the wood ranch house in which she currendy lives around 1969, after renting the home for two years. With the way the children ate, they were not able to save much money. Then there were clothing expenses. By the time Carl retired, Kathleen estimates that he made about $60,000 annually. And sixty thousand dollars is an attractive income in her area of the country.

Although they never had much savings, they made one financial move that, in retrospect, Kathleen says really helped. They took out life insurance policies on their children when they were very young. "They were good and cheap."

With a cash value policy, the couple paid a periodic premium. Part of the money covered the death benefits, and the other part went into a savings account that earned a rate return set by the insurance company. The savings protection is called the cash value of a life insurance policy. Insurance companies let policyholders borrow against the cash value in their policy tax-free, often at unusually low rates. Of course, the death benefits are reduced by the outstanding loan balance and accumulated interest.

When the children got old enough to drive, they were able to borrow money on the policies for their first cars, but they had to pay it back. The children also paid for their own gas and insurance. One daughter, who went to college, had worked at the same company as Carl. The company covered major college expenses, as a special benefit for children of its employees.

The couple also had a top-notch medical insurance plan through Carl's job. Plus, Carl had life insurance and a pension. Nevertheless, because both spouses had been so ill, Kathleen was left with $47,000 in hospital bills after Carl died, over and above what his life insurance policy covered. The 20 percent that's not covered by the insurance company can really add up when two people are gravely ill. With all those bills, there was little left for her to carry on.

The good news was that the three-bedroom, 2,300-square-foot ranch house she had lived in was completely paid off two years after her husband died.

"I took care of the money when he traveled," she says." I knew what we owed. I knew how to pay bills and write checks." Both spouses' names had been on their accounts.

After Carl died, Kathleen got part of his pension, his social security, and her own social security disability because of her cancer. But today that often isn't enough.

Although after Carl died expenses seemed tight, Kathleen's mother was aging and on a walker. The two got along well, so

Kathleen suggested that she move in. Her mother, who had a railroad pension, offered to pay $200 monthly for room and board. The added money came as a welcome relief. Often Kathleen's brothers, who live six hours from her, visited and gave her some respite as she cared for her mother. Kathleen's youngest son also lived with her for a while. When her mother was forced to use a wheelchair, Kathleen bought a 1990 Pontiac Trans Sport and often drove her to see family. Finally, her mother could no longer walk and Kathleen could no longer take care of her alone. She was forced to put her in a nursing home. "That," she says, "was the hardest thing I ever had to do."

When her mother went on Medicaid around the turn of the century, Kathleen not only had to deal with the grief of putting a parent in a nursing home, but she also lost important income from her mother's monthly pension checks. She was totally on her own.

"I had to worry when the taxes were due," she says. "I could eke out the groceries. I was never destitute. I could pay my bills. But I really had to watch that I wasn't buying any extra toiletries—-just my basic stuff." The van, which was getting older, started needing more repairs. Although her son was able to do many of the repairs, she still had to order costly parts.

She estimates that she currently gets $1,200 monthly— including Social Security and disability income, and $225 monthly from an annuity that her husband had through his job.

Her property taxes alone ran close to $2,000 in 2002. Her health insurance, through Cenex, runs $250 monthly, and she pays a man to mow her yard. She also is on Medicare. "It was getting tough to pay taxes or a car repair that would come up," she says. There were no phone calls from creditors. If that ever happened, "I would have a heart attack," she says.

Kathleen faces a problem many newly retired people face. Year by year, the dollar buys less. Meanwhile, health-care and drug costs keep rising.

It is especially tough on senior citizens. You don't want to be forced into borrowing money on credit cards. That's a surefire way to go bankrupt. You can't work due to an illness. And you don't want to ask friends and family for money. It's embarrassing. Plus, they are hard-pressed, too.

Kathleen had heard about reverse mortgages on television and had several friends who were Realtors. With a reverse mortgage, you borrow money based upon the equity you have in your home. Although it can work similarly to a home equity loan or home equity credit line, the difference is that you never have to pay it off unless you move, sell the home, or die. It sounded like a good deal. She asked friends who were knowledgeable about a reverse mortgage and got a couple of names. "I don't need to worry about getting screwed," she says. To qualify for a reverse mortgage, she was required to be 62. She turned that age in September 2002, so she went to Intermoun-tain Mortgage Co. in Billings, Montana.

In addition to Financial Freedom, her mortgage documents carry phone numbers for HUD and Fannie Mae. "There are a lot of players in this thing," she notes of the reverse mortgage application process. They want to make sure nobody's doing anything they shouldn't be doing. They sent me papers and said if I didn't get my money in a certain amount of time, I should call this number." She started the application process September 12, 2002, and estimates that there were about five visits back to the mortgage company. "They had to explain everything to me," she says. "Everybody had to know that I wasn't getting taken."

Different types of reverse mortgages were available. She opted for a line of credit. "I don't draw on it," she says. "I leave it there. If I don't use it, I don't have to pay for it." Her house was appraised at $118,000.

The original principal she is permitted to withdraw from the reverse mortgage was $72,000. If she needs to draw on the credit line, she sends in a special form to Financial Freedom; within five business days, the money is automatically deposited in her checking account. If she requests more than $10,000, her request must be verified. At this writing, Kathleen has drawn down about $35,000, although she has not tapped it all. She says she used the money so far to pay for an $800 car repair bill and a $6,000 credit card bill. She estimates that another $5,000 is held in reserve to cover the fees for the reverse mortgage. She keeps the rest of her advance in a savings account, just in case she needs it. She still holds the deed on the property, and if she doesn't use up the rest of her credit line, her children can inherit whatever equity she has left in her home.

Kathleen realized she would be taking her children's inheritance. She discussed it with her children. "If I could leave that to my kids, it would be wonderful," she says. "But if I could live my life a little better, I felt I should do that. My kids told me to go for it! They were thrilled."

Today Kathleen credits a reverse mortgage with allowing her to finally reap some rewards from her retired life. Normally, her trips to visit her large family, made up of nine brothers and sisters, have consisted of a long drive. She was the driver. Often she brought along her mother, who was confined to a wheelchair. When we talked with Kathleen, her mother, in her 90s, was in a nursing home. Her health had begun to deteriorate. For the last two trips, Kathleen, traveling alone, was able to fly for the first time. "It was just good and relaxing not to have to think about anything. I didn't have to worry about what the weather was doing," she says.

The trips provided a badly needed break. "They took me sightseeing," she says of her first trip to her sister. "We went out to eat and went to estate sales." Antiques are her passion. "I don't buy a lot. I just look," she stresses. For $30, she picked up a very old set of poetry books. They were in good shape. Authors included Thomas Gray, John Keats, Lord Byron, and William Blake, which she was looking forward to reading. 'Just being with the family was neat."

Everyone thought she was crazy when she visited North Dakota on her second trip, she admits. 'You don't have enough snow where you are, kid?" they asked her. But it was worth it to see her other sister, who, like her, is a widow. "We went antiquing there, too," she says. "There's an old candy store that we always go to when we go there. We always get a little baggie of candy. We've been going there for 50 years. It's kind of fun."

Kathleen says that although she has access to $72,000, she is trying to be very frugal. But she was happy with the process of applying for the reverse mortgage. "It was an easy process— a lot of paperwork," she says, estimating that there were some 300 pages to go through. "There's nothing I would do differently."

She now has the best of both worlds. She feels financially secure. She is watching her money closely and hopes to leave some to her children when she is no longer around. But she knows that if she has to tap the cash over the years, it is there.

The reverse mortgage was an easy financial move for Kathleen to take. She is using her paid-off home as a source of income. Plus, she doesn't have to leave the home she has lived in for most of her life.

Worry-free, she now spends a great deal of time with her eight grandchildren. "I love that!" she says. "When I feel up to it, I go to the nursing home every other day—usually. But I really haven't had much time. I've had so much company coming to see their mom and all my brothers and sisters."

She says she keeps one credit card—the same one she had with her husband. "I use that for flying or whatever. I don't have to use it for anything else." By not using it, she spends less money. People are less likely to buy on impulse if they have to reach into the wallet or purse and pull out money, she says; they realize the cost of goods and services when they don't use the charge card.

"Right now, I watch it," she says. "I do not worry about money. I don't go out and throw it around. If I can get it cheaper somewhere else, I wouldn't just go buy it. But I don't budget, per se. If I want to go out for lunch, I do. Then I have protein and salad. For dinner, I might have a piece of toast; I don't spend too much on food. When I want, I buy one little steak. One pork chop will feed me two meals."

Doing It Yourself

If you're at least 62 years old, like Kathleen, you might have an easier life, thanks to the availability of reverse mortgages. But don't be fooled. A reverse mortgage is a fancy term for a loan. In fact, if anything, reverse mortgages may prove more costly than other types of loans. Reverse mortgages charge interest and come complete with many of the same types of fees that you find on a traditional mortgage, such as an application fee, closing costs, a survey, inspections, recording fees, and mortgage taxes. You also might expect to find a "risk-pooling" or "reverse mortgage insurance" premium and a servicing fee. You can opt to get your reverse mortgage loan as a credit line or in a lump sum—much like a home equity loan or line of credit. Or, you can get it in a combination of ways.

The chief difference between a reverse mortgage and a traditional mortgage loan is that you do not have to repay the reverse mortgage loan or credit line until you move, sell the home, or die. Instead, the loan balance, which includes all your cash advances, fees, and interest, is repaid from the equity of your home. The amount that you or your heirs can owe, however, is limited by the home's value when the loan is repaid. You don't necessarily need any income to qualify for a reverse mortgage, either. That's because you needn't make any payments. The amount that you can borrow generally is based on your age, your home's value and location, and the cost of your loan.

At this writing, there were four major issuers of reverse mortgages:

- The Federal Housing Administration (FHA) of the U.S. Department of Housing and Urban Development (HUD), Washington, D.C., at www.hud.gov or 800-569-4287
- Federal National Mortgage Association (Fannie Mae), at www.fanniemae.com or 800-732-6643
- Financial Freedom Senior Funding Corp., Irvine, California, at www.ffsenior.com or 800-500-5150
- Canadian Home Income Plan (CHIP) Corp., Toronto, Ontario, Canada, at www.chip.ca or 800-563-2447

However, some of these programs may be offered through mortgage brokers nationally.

More than 95 percent of all the reverse mortgages made nationally are federally insured mortgages issued by the Federal Housing Authority, says Ken Scholen, a reverse mortgage specialist with the AARP, formerly the American Association of Retired Persons. With this program, the size of your loan is limited based on your geographic area. In 2003, it ranged from a low of $154,896 to a high of $280,749.

In most cases, Scholen says, FHA's home equity conversion mortgage is the best deal of the nationally available reverse mortgage programs. "The odds are way against it that you'll get a lot of money out of (Fannie Mae's) Homekeeper (reverse mortgage) than the (FHA) home equity conversion mortgage," he says. The Financial Freedom "cash account" generally works out to be best if your home value is $500,000 or greater, he adds.

However, to make certain that you are getting the best program for your needs, you can go online to an excellent calculator at www.rmaarp.com.

Considering a reverse mortgage? Scholen suggests that you first look at the prospect of selling your home and moving. "Find out how much you could get for your house and look at other places you might live," he advises. You might be surprised at how much you could get for your house, or you might be surprised to know the alternative living arrangements that are available.

Next, he suggests, check to see whether any state or local governments in your area offer a very low-cost reverse mortgage for a specific purpose. In some areas, he says, there may be special reverse mortgage programs available to pay property taxes or to make a home repair. If you can find these types of programs, they actually might be your lowest-cost option.

Learn as much as you can before you shop for a reverse mortgage, Scholen adds. Mandatory reading before considering a reverse mortgage can be found at www.reverse.org. Or, you can call a toll-free number, 1-800-209-8085, for a free brochure. Also visit the website of the National Reverse Mortgage Lenders Association atwww.reversemortgage.org. If you know as much as possible about a reverse mortgage in advance, you'll know the right questions to ask when you go into counseling, Scholen says.

Always get counseling for a reverse mortgage program— regardless of whether it's mandatory, Scholen suggests. Generally the counseling, offered in conjunction with the U.S. Department of Housing and Urban Development is free or very low cost. You can get a list of approved counseling agencies through www.reverse.org.

"Seriously consider involving your heirs in the whole process," Scholen says. Too many homeowners simply don't want to talk this decision over with anyone else. However, if you talk to family members first, "it could be the first time the family hears you're having trouble financially," he says. "Sometimes other solutions can come out of that."

If you do obtain a reverse mortgage, beware that they typically have adjustable rates. So if the rate looks attractive now, it could rise in the future.

One final thing to be considered: If you are on low-income supplemental security income (SSI) or Medicaid, you must be particularly careful not to draw any more from your reverse mortgage loan or credit line in any given month than you actually need to spend. If you deposit any excess money into a bank account, it could be added to your other assets, jeopardizing your federal benefits.

Chapter 12

Vicki and Paul Terhorst: A New Breed of Retiree-Perpetual Travelers

Unless you really love your job, anyone would be inspired by the story of Paul Terhorst and his wife, Vicki. The couple retired in their mid-30s with a net worth of less than $500,000. We first read about the childless couple in 1988. Paul had left a plum job as a fast-rising partner for Peat, Marwick, Mitchell, now KPMG, in California. Vicki had never made more than $20,000 annually as an artist and educator. Yet, the two did what many their age had merely hoped to do.

They chucked their quarter-million-dollar San Francisco condo, maid and high-pressure lifestyle to move to Argentina. As we wrote this chapter, the two were much older. Paul was 54 and Vicki was 53. Yet, they have been reincarnated into a new breed of retiree. With no home other than an e-mail address on a computer, they constantly travel the world as "perpetual travelers," or, as they say for short, "PTs."

As Paul wrote in his best-selling business book *Cashing in on the American Dream: How to Retire at 35.* (Bantam, 1988), it all started with a decision to sell assets, (including their home), put money in high-rate bank certificates of deposit (at the time), and moved to a lower-cost area.

Leaving San Francisco, one of the nation's most expensive cities, was a smart move for this young retired couple. After all, a San Francisco lifestyle that required $110,000 in annual income would require less than half that much in cities such as Louisville, Kentucky; New Orleans, Louisiana; Houston, Texas; and Virginia Beach, Virginia.

The couple, however, chose an even cheaper route. They headed to the Buenos Aires area of Argentina. It was so cheap to live that they bought a one-bedroom condo with a balcony near the beach for just $20,000. It cost the couple just $40 a month. That covered property taxes, maintenance, condo fees, utilities, and insurance. Meanwhile, they kept their money in laddered U.S. CDs—then earning 8 percent—and belonged to a low-cost Argentinean health maintenance organization (HMO).

At first, living in an area with a low cost of living helped make the couple's retirement a reality. For a number of years, their HMO coverage was dirt cheap. (Today they self-insure using health care outside the United States.)

While living in Argentina, they kept their money in one-year CDs that matured monthly at various banks. According to *Forbes* magazine, the strategy produced $22,220 in annual income. Their initial retirement funds were reported to have come from Paul's Peat Marwick buyout, the sale of four investment apartments in California, and savings. They spent three to six months at their home base, and the rest of the year traveling.

Eventually, the Terhorsts' retirement stash grew to about $850,000, which included $50,000 from Paul's book, for which he received a $9,000 advance. As CD rates dropped in half— from the 8 percent at the time he wrote the book to 4 percent— the couple moved a little more than half of their money into stocks and the rest in bonds and cash.

As we were completing this chapter in early 2003, the couple's assets had grown to more than $1 million, according to *Kiplinger's Personal Finance* magazine. They had "40 percent of their holdings in large and small company stocks, 40 percent in natural resource companies (oil, gold, platinum), and the rest in money market accounts," *Kiplinger's* reported. Although assets might have been down in the bear market from their peak, Paul was unconcerned about the three-year bear market. He was getting ready to collect his pension.

They decided to leave Argentina in 1991 when inflation began spiraling out of control. "Our apartment expenses quadrupled," Paul wrote in Escapeartist.com of their life in that country. "But the main reason we wanted to get rid of the apartment and become perpetual travelers (PTs) was because we were tired of returning to the same place every year ...."

It did not seem as though they were true PTs initially, based on when *Money* magazine caught up with them in 1993. Then they seemed to have laid roots in Austin, Texas, where they were renting a one-bedroom apartment for $435 monthly.

Besides offering the couple cheap rent at the time, Texas was one of the few states with no personal income tax. *Money* says the couple spent $4,000 annually traveling and maintained an HMO membership in Argentina at a cost of $100 annually. The HMO was intended only for major medical care. Apart from that, the Terhorsts were paying their own medical costs.

They wound up abandoning their Texas home base entirely. They also did away with their HMO coverage. The couple felt that with a net worth of more than half a million dollars, they had enough money to self-insure, as long as they obtained their health care outside the United States.

The couple says that they tested their medical insurance strategy. One of them was hospitalized in Argentina, Guatemala, and France and visited emergency rooms in Argentina, Guatemala, and Thailand. "We have had excellent primary care physicians in Argentina, Mexico, Thailand, and France," the two wrote.

So how do they find good doctors overseas? In Paul's book, he claims that their philosophy largely is to talk to people and get recommendations.

"Our experience is that Americans can find high-quality medical care abroad if they use good judgment, have the right attitude, and exercise a little caution," Paul wrote after Vicki had tripped and broken her foot some 300 miles outside Buenos Aires.

In their travels, the Terhorsts shun expensive American hotels, opting instead to go a bit out of the way to stay in cheaper locally run hotels that they often find by word of mouth. They pay only for the services they need, avoiding luxuries such as elevators, swimming pools and air-conditioning.

Do without a car, if possible, they advise. Find a great travel agent who knows how to find you the best travel deals. Paul recommends establishing your address in a place that has no state income tax.

Paul's mailing address is at his brother's home, in Washington. His brother tosses his mail in a box. When Paul asks for something, he sends it.

The couple also has a travel computer. They have data files that include names and addresses; a list of the contents and locations of their storage boxes; important information such as credit cards, passport numbers, and birthdays; and bank and broker information. When they get to a printer, they print out the files—six pages, copied on both sides of paper. They've reported that they visit parents and siblings periodically in the United States. But they don't make more than a couple of long distance calls monthly. They go online, when possible at libraries and Internet cafes.

While traveling, the couple use Visa or MasterCard debit cards, which can be used either in ATMs or in banks for good exchange rates. The Terhorsts are very outspoken against using travelers' checks or credit cards. The reason: They're too expensive.

If you go on the road, your investments must be safe yet must earn a solid rate of return. That means you have little option but to invest part of your holdings in stocks as a hedge against inflation. Historically, stocks have earned about 7 percent more than the inflation rate. You also can invest in bonds and cash investments such as CDs for income.

On the stock side, the Terhorsts have said they have invested in low-cost index stock funds. Index funds invest in a basket of stocks such as 500 large-company stocks that make up the S&P 500 stock index. Their expenses generally are cheaper than those of actively managed funds, which can make a major difference in the returns you earn. Index funds charge expenses ranging from .20 percent to .5 percent. By contrast, the average actively managed common stock fund charges 1.5 percent annually.

The Terhorsts don't believe in avoiding all countries with dictatorships or in skipping a country just because there is some turmoil. Sometimes, they say, turmoil can work in your favor. Take the time in 1989, when Argentina had massive inflation. Paul had seen a pair of tennis shoes for 2000 pesos or $20. By the time he got to the store, the shoes cost the

Vicki and Paul Terhorst: A New Breed of Retiree-Perpetual Travelers

equivalent of $10. In the additional short time it took him to change his money, the price of the shoes had dropped to $3.

They also have admitted that at times, money has been tight. But Vicki strongly believes that by maintaining a positive attitude, you can gain control of your negative thought patterns.

Of course, retiring today is a different ball game than it was in the 1980s and 1990s. For one thing, it costs more to live in many countries than the couple initially spent. At first, their goal was to keep their costs averaging less than $50 a day.

Today, they acknowledge, that budget is tough to meet in some areas. Also, the stock market lost 40 percent over the first three years of the new millennium. Today it is hard to find a federally insured bank certificate of deposit (CD) yielding more than 3 to 4 percent.

Fortunately, it appears that they have succeeded in growing their assets. Even if things would have failed to go well, Paul has always believed that once you retire, you can always go back to work. In fact, he appears to be working slightly—at least. We found him listed as a columnist for *International Living* magazine. One essay at his website also referred to the fact that he has a press pass to a fashion show. So, we also assume that the perk of a press pass gains the couple free access to some things, cutting some of their bills. The couple's website indicates that they are enjoying their travels around the world.

Paul and Vicki are the only ones in this book who declined our request for an interview. "Thanks for asking," Vicki e-mailed. "However, we have no interest in being profiled for the book." We later found an indication of their sentiment at their website, www.goecities.com/The Tropics/Shores/5315, in response to a question on whether they thought about updating their book. They have, and publishers have been interested, they say. "However, the market for this kind of book is still small, rewriting is a lot of work, and promotion is not as much fun anymore."

From our research, we discovered that the couple have developed quite a cult following of early retirees. It also was tough to find their book, now out of print, for less than $40— that's used! Much of our research on early retirees also cited their book as a major source of inspiration. And in 1988, Paul Terhorst held the distinction of appearing on the cover of *Money* magazine and its chief rival, *Changing Times* (now

Kiplinger's Personal Finance), in the same month. So, we couldn't help but wonder, did they take the right strategy? Are they still happy? We decided to do some of our own research.

Yes, they are still happy, they actually responded quite recently on their website. "Every year gets easier and better," Vicki says. "Because we are open to opportunities and because we know what makes us happy, we are able to both direct our lives while going with the flow."

She notes, however, that what the couple will be doing five years from now is a mystery. "The mystery of how our lives evolve is part of the fun and adventure."

Keeping active while saving money is important when you retire. You need to keep busying with meaningful things to do. But you should do things that are not expensive.

Paul recommends that in retirement, you make a "to-do" list. Initially, his included riding bikes, learning yoga and transcendental meditation, playing golf, and cooking. Upon his retirement, he took up playing the saxophone. He also wrote an unpublished novel. Vicki, a vegetarian, had taken up New Age crystals and spiritual healing.

You can do plenty of things. Gandhi once said, "You should live your life as if you are going to die tomorrow. You should learn like you are going to live forever."

Take some classes in subjects that interest you. Learn a foreign language. Go to art and book discussions. Enjoy the excitement of local sporting events. Meet people in discussion groups. Get involved with volunteer work.

Paul also advises using computers. They can be helpful in corresponding with friends, tracking investments, and getting news.

According to their website, the Terhorsts currently travel the world. They research areas to visit on the Internet and still return to places they love. They live cheaply, managing to find low-cost sources of entertainment—and they thoroughly enjoy the adventure. Taking 8-mile walks, playing tennis, and visiting with the numerous friends they have hooked up with through their web page and travels are just a few of their pastimes. They also frequent museums and libraries and take cooking classes. While in France, they note, their third greatest monthly expense was a daily cup of espresso in a local cafe.

The Terhorsts have succeeded in making retiring early a science. They watch every penny. Here are some of the keys to their success:

- They cut their housing costs by downsizing to a one-bedroom apartment in a warm climate. Utility costs, if you watch your air conditioning bills, are lower than in cold climes, where the cost of heating oil can run a few hun dred dollars monthly in the dead of winter. Going without air conditioning didn't bother them.
- They tried to locate near shopping and public transporta tion. They prefer areas where they don't need a car. They also avoid taking taxis. They buy transit passes in large cities like Paris. They also buy rail passes to travel to differ ent countries.
- They travel with no belongings or appliances and limit themselves to apartments with one bedroom and one bath.
- They took cooking classes, and avoided high-priced restaurants.
- They rent movies and watch television, avoiding the high prices of movie theaters.
- They get to know the locals when they move to an overseas area. Entertaining often consists of socializing. They rely on the locals rather than institutions to give them advice on where to eat, where to stay and where to find reasonably priced health care.
- They go to local festivals.
- They travel off-season when costs are lower. They take advantage of slow times to get the best prices. The tourist, for example, goes to the Yucatan peninsula in the winter. But no one is there in the summer. Of course, to do this, you need to be comfortable in hot weather.
- They travel to countries where the currency is weak. Make sure you live in areas where prices are based on local currencies—not the U.S. dollar. Avoid tourist areas like the plague.
- They rent apartments instead of owning. This avoids legal problems and risks due to foreign currency.

- They stay in native hotels if they are in an area for a short time. For example, in 1998, when they visited Southeast Asia, they were able to find hotels for just a couple of dollars a day.
- They keep their expenses on par with their investment income. Although initially, they had budgeted $50 a day, today, they say, you can live on that amount in Mexico, but not necessarily in Europe.
- They keep physically fit. The advice on their website: Spend an hour daily taking care of your teeth. Stretch your back a half-hour daily. Do some type of aerobic exercise for an hour daily. Meditate an hour daily. Practice yoga an hour daily.

Doing It Yourself

One problem that any retiree faces is making money last. Younger retirees who live on a shoestring still need to make their money grow over the years. Experts say it is a good idea for them to keep at least 50 percent in stocks if they are in their 50s. Most likely, they will be living well into their 80s. If inflation grows at 3 percent annual rate, a 50-year-old who purchased $100 worth of groceries today would have to pay $209 for the same food at age 75.

The Terhorsts are having a good time traveling the world. But they must ensure that their nest egg keeps growing by getting the best return on their investments with the least amount of risk.

Consider Index Funds

If you can't beat the stock market, why not join it? The Terhorsts made a smart move investing in index funds, which track the performance of the overall stock market. The S&P 500 Index is made up of 500 of the largest, most profitable blue-chip companies traded on the stock exchange.

Over the past 15 years, for example, the Vanguard 500 Index Fund has outperformed 83 percent of all stock funds, according to Morningstar Inc., Chicago. Meanwhile, the Vanguard Total Market Fund, which tracks all the stocks traded on the New York, American and NASDAQ stock exchanges, has outperformed 81 percent of all stock funds.

The major reasons: Index funds are low-cost. Their annual expenses are at least one percent less than those of actively managed stock funds.

With a 1 percent difference in expenses, a $10,000 investment earning 10 percent over 10 years in a lower-cost index fund could net you nearly $2,000 more—$24,782 versus 22,610.

In addition to generally being low-cost, stock index funds have outperformed almost 70 percent of actively managed stock funds over the past 15 years, based on Morningstar data.

Cutting Expenses

The Terhorsts seem to have a system that works. It may be harder to retire in your mid-30s today, even with a half-million dollars, but it can be done. You've got to zero in on cutting your expenses to the bone while maximizing your retirement income.

You'd be surprised how much you can save over one year's time. Write down everything you spend money on during the month. Only then can you really see where it goes.

Jonathan Pond's book *1001 Ways to Cut Your Expenses* (Dell, 1992) is a fun, easy-to-read book full of cost-cutting tips. Among the biggest wastes of your money that he lists are these:

- Playing the lottery
- Buying a new car every few years
- Buying credit life insurance
- Investing on the advice of someone you've never met
- Going to fancy restaurants
- Buying something on sale that you don't need
- Taking out credit card loans
- Lending money to friends
- Buying designer-label clothing

Save money traveling the world by purchasing an international health insurance policy, which can cost half as much as U.S. coverage for the same benefits. Be careful though. Policies probably don't cover treatment in the United States.

Airfare can be a major expense when you are retired and living on a fixed income. But if you have access to a computer, you can cut your costs traveling the world.

Sign up to be alerted about special deals at websites like Orbitz.com, Expedia.com, and Travelocity.com. Websites of major airlines and cruise ship lines also let you sign up for travel alerts.

Consider checking Sidestep.com for a search of some 140 websites for the lowest travel prices. Other sites to consider: Hotwire.com and Priceline.com. But be careful. With Priceline. com, you type in where you want to go and how much you'd like to pay. If your request is accepted, the charge automatically is put through on your credit card. Hotwire.com, by contrast, gives you an hour to decide whether to accept its offer.

There are other ways to cut fares. You might leave from alternative airports. For example, it's cheaper to leave from Providence, Rhode Island than from Logan Airport in Boston. Websites, like Bestfares.com, can check alternative sites for you.

You often can get cheaper fares if you stay over on a Saturday. Off-hour flight times also may be less expensive. At this writing, Tuesdays were said to be the slowest airline travel day.

Check airline websites or travel agents for last minute tickets. Other websites to visit for airline deals: WebFlyer.com and TravelZoo.com.

The Terhorsts stress in dieir book that those who retire young can save money by living like students. Students live cheaply by avoiding high-priced restaurants, clipping supermarket store coupons, and going to places in groups to lower expenses.

You also can wear simple and inexpensive clothes, like jeans and T-shirts. Perhaps you might consider sharing living space with other people.

You might consider living in warm-weather states like Texas and Florida. Not only do you save money on clothes, but those states also have no state income taxes. This can save as much as 8 percent of your investment income.

On the heath insurance side, you can lower your cost if you are not eligible for Medicare. Choosing a high deductible cuts your monthly health insurance premiums substantially. If you are in good health, why pay the insurance company up front?

Look for the lowest-cost type of plan. Depending upon the state you live in, an indemnity policy can cost much less than a managed-care program. With an indemnity policy, you can go to any doctor you like. With managed care, you must deal with the network of doctors that belong to the program.

Indemnity policies typically have a deductible and pay 75 to 80 percent of your medical bills after you've reached your deductible. Most plans have an out-of-pocket maximum. For example, after you have incurred $5,000 in medical expenses, your indemnity policy may pay 100 percent.

Some simple preventative steps can reduce future heath-care costs. Taking these steps can save you thousand of dollars over the years. For example:
- Don't smoke.
- Don't drink alcohol excessively.
- If you're overweight, lose the extra weight and keep it off.
- Exercise regularly.
- Brush and floss your teeth daily.
- Get an annual physical check-up.
- Use sun block.
- Check out services at dental and medical schools.
- Buy generic drugs.
- Eat plenty of fruits and vegetables, as well as foods that are high in fiber.
- Avoid eating junk food that is high in fat and cholesterol. * Get a good night's sleep.
- Consider meditation.

Send Your Children to Public Schools

If you need to save more for your retirement, consider steering your children toward state universities rather than private universities.

For the 2002-2003 school year, tuition at a four-year public school averaged just $4,081 annually. That's less than one-quarter of the annual cost—$18,273—at a private school, according to the College Board, Princeton, New Jersey.

Experts say that corporations today no longer are as concerned as they once were that a degree comes from an Ivy League university.

In fact, Dawn Towe, a recruiter for Target Corporation told *The New York Times* in 2002 that private college students often have "unrealistic expectations" about their ability to rise quickly in a company. Too often, she said, they want to be in charge of marketing from the onset.

Are You Ready to Retire Early?

So have the Terhorsts inspired you to retire early?

Take this quiz designed by Helen Dennis, a retirement consultant with the Andrus Gerontology Center, University of Southern California. You will learn whether you have the money and state of mind to do it. You may circle more than one answer.

1. To be sure you have sufficient income in retirement you have ...
   A. Written down the income and benefits you will get from your employer and Social Security.
   B. Calculated your expected retirement income.
   C. Estimated your retirement expenses.
   D. None of the above.

2. Do you save for retirement in the following accounts?
   A. IRA, Keogh or SEP.
   B. 401 (k) or 403 (b) plan.
   C. Stocks, bonds, mutual funds, and other investments.
   D. None of the above.

3. How would you feel if you stopped working today?
   A. Financially secure.
   B. Happy not having to work.
   C. Feel like you are unworthy.

4. What would you do if you had a week off?
   A. Have fun at home.
   B. Travel.
   C. Be anxious to get back to work.

5. Are you currently doing the following?
   A. Volunteer work.
   B. Member of a club or organization.
   C. Engaged in a group activity outside of work.
   D. None of the above.

6. What do you do to stay healthy?
   A. Regularly exercise.
   B. Keep a low-fat, high carbohydrate diet.
   C. Deal with stress well.
   D. None of the above.

7. Have you ...
   A. Talked to someone who retired early?
   B. Not talked to someone who retired early?

8. How do you expect to pay for medical costs until you reach 65 and become eligible for Medicare?
   A. You plan to get medical coverage through an insurance policy with your employer.
   B. You plan to buy health insurance yourself.
   C. You don't know.

9. Do you plan to earn extra income when you retire?
   A. You plan to learn new skills before you retire.
   B. You have a hobby you can turn into a job.
   C. You will do the same work you do now, but plan to do it on your schedule.
   D. You don't know.

10. What does your spouse or partner think of your plan to retire early?
    A. He or she thinks it is a great idea.
    B. He or she is looking forward to spending more time together.
    C. He or she probably would climb the walls if you retired early.

How to score your quiz. If you don't have enough money, you can't retire early. Give yourself 2 points for answers A, B, or C but no points for D for the first two questions. For all other questions, give yourself 1 point for each circled answer except for the last one in each set, which gets zero.

If you score is 1 to 13 points, you are not ready for early retirement. You must start preparing for it.

If you score 14 to 22 points, you could retire early. But you need to save more and keep healthy.

If you score 23 points or more, you can retire early. You have the money and the state of mind to stop working and enjoy life.

This test helps you find out where you are in terms of retirement. Once you take it, you can make changes with the goal of retiring earlier than you think.

Epilogue

So you'd really like to retire, but you don't have much money. Or, perhaps you had plenty of money but saw it eroded in the recent bear market. Now your retirement is in question. What can you do?

The gracious people in *Rags to Retirement* might have provided us with some insight.

Among the tickets to retirement that they have suggested are these:

- Find a cheaper way to live. Tom Murphy lives on a sailboat with a home base in Boston. Alan and Sandy Clark moved into a recreational vehicle. Neither vehicle requires payment of property taxes. The Schraders and the Plunketts moved to other lower-cost countries. The Monfortes moved to a low-cost area in Florida.
- Cut your medical expenses. You can do this in the United States by self-insuring. In other words, increase your medical insurance deductible to $2,500 or so, and be sure to stay healthy. This involves exercising and eating properly. You also might consider cutting medical expenses simply by living in another country. As we've learned from many of our subjects, the United States has one of the world's most expensive health-care systems.
- Plan for your retirement at a young age. The Ferstenous started planning for their retirement in their 20s. As a result, they were able to take advantage of many years of an appreciating stock market.
- Obtain a job with great retirement and/or medical benefits. Alex Monforte had his retirement standard of living boosted substantially by the pension he obtained from his job at the United Nations. Tom Murphy was also helped dramatically by the defined benefit plan he obtained while working at the U.S. Postal Service.

- Set goals for yourself. Even in retirement, having a clear goal can keep you on track and maintain your sense of well-being. The Marks, despite their misfortunes, are looking forward to the day when their dream retirement home is completed. And Dennis Hastings worked toward the goal of someday having a museum-interpretive center for Omaha tribal members.
- Become more social. Getting together with friends and family is a cheap, yet extremely fulfilling form of entertainment. Do this when you're young instead of eating out in restaurants and partaking of other expensive activities, and you'll have more money to put away for your retirement. You also can cut your retirement expenses dramatically if you spend time with people rather than spend money on costly activities. Perhaps a simple change in what you do for entertainment is all that you truly need to retire comfortably.
- Take advantage of free or low-cost sources of entertainment. Libraries and museums can offer entertaining, educational, and cheap forms of entertainment. Also consider local outdoor concerts and festivities.
- Make the most of federal benefits to which you might be entitled. Federally subsidized housing, social security, supplemental security income, Veterans Administration benefits, and shared housing programs might be ways to improve your lifestyle in retirement. Familiarize yourself with these options, and take advantage of them as necessary. Know your consumer rights.
- Do repairs or construction yourself rather than hiring out help. Once you're retired, you have the time to learn these tasks. Duane Mark decided to use his career as a carpenter to his advantage. He is building his dream retirement home. Tom Murphy does most of his boat repairs himself. And Alex Monforte says he does most of the household tasks on his own.
- As you near retirement, invest conservatively in insured or federally guaranteed investments. This way, you needn't

worry about a bear market hurting your nest egg just when you're likely to need it.
- Cut taxes as much as possible. Consider relocating to a state that has no income tax (Florida, Texas, Alaska, South Dakota, Washington, Wyoming, or Nevada).
- Get rid of your car, if possible. You'll save as much as $7,754 annually, according to the American Automobile Association. That includes gas, oil, maintenance, tires, insurance, depreciation, licenses, registration, taxes, and finances charges on a new car loan.
- Consider a reverse mortgage. If you own a home, a reverse mortgage might be a way to extract income from it, while not having to worry about paying it back. Kathleen Maddox reports that, for her, a reverse mort gage marked the beginning of her financial freedom.
- Maintain a positive attitude. Dennis Hastings and the Marks are among those who proved that thinking posi tively can get you through the worst of times.

As you've probably gathered, it is harder for many to retire today than was for previous generations.

For one thing, the age at which people may be eligible for Social Security benefits is rising. In fact, many were questioning whether Social Security and Medicare benefits would even be around by the time the baby boomers and subsequent generations need them. The bear market that took hold in 2000 and continued as we wrote this book hasn't helped.

While combing the country for persons with attractive lifestyles, we noticed that finding a low-cost place to live is getting harder. Persons in low-cost trailer parks were constantly being threatened with having to leave as developers considered selling land. Municipalities were constantly trying to prohibit liveaboards on boats. And rent control in many areas was getting phased out. Pair all these factors with rising health-care costs, and it could prove very difficult for prospective retirees to make that final commitment to quit their jobs and live the good life. We will say, however, that although many of those we interviewed had lost money in the stock market, not one single person regretted the move to retire—even those who retired early.

Alan and Sandy Clark, in fact, told us that they were very happy they made their decision to retire in a recreational vehicle before the market tanked. This spared them much of the turmoil prospective retirees are experiencing now. Kathleen Maddox, a widow, offered some strong words of advice: Travel when you're young, she said.

We had a very difficult time finding people to interview for this book as the stock market was plummeting. The reason: More people seemed to be going back to work than seemed to be retiring. At least two people we thought would have great stories told us that they were going back to work—which, incidentally, is nothing to be ashamed about, once you've retired.

We also found that, in some cases, poor health had made the lives of formerly happy and creative retirees extraordinarily difficult. One gentleman we had hoped to interview suddenly found himself as caregiver to his wife, who was too ill to take care of herself.

Regrettably, these are some of the realities that future retirees someday will have to face. That is why we hoped to present some of these situations to you in our book. It proved that even persons who must deal with adversity can find creative ways to cope.

We tried very hard to provide you with as many different creative lifestyles as we could find. However, despite all our hard work, only you can decide whether it's time to retire and which is the right lifestyle for you.

We hope that our book opened your mind to some new ideas and that it will inspire you to find your own creative way to retire.

About Gail Liberman and Alan Lavine

Gail Liberman and Alan Lavine are husband-and-wife columnists and best-selling authors based in Palm Beach Gardens, Florida.

Their columns run in the *Boston Herald, Pittsburgh Post-Gazette, Palm Beach Daily News,* several Scripps Howard newspapers, America Online, CNBC.com, MyFinancialAdvisor.com Fundsinteractive.com, Allaboutfunds.com, and Quicken.com.

Liberman and Lavine's book *Rags to Riches: Motivating Stories of How Ordinary People Achieved Extraordinary Wealth!* (Dearborn, 2000) was featured on Oprah and hit two best-seller lists.

You may have seen or heard the couple on television and radio. They have been guests on CBS's *The Early Show,* CNN, CNBC, *The 700 Club,* and PBS. They also have been quoted in

The Wall Street Journal, Money Magazine, USA Today, The New York Times, Business Week, Investors Business Daily, The Washington Post, Redbook, First, Town and Country, Bride's, and *Elle.*

Their other books are *Love, Marriage and Money* (Dearborn, 1998), *The Complete Idiot's Guide to Making Money with Mutual Funds* (Alpha Books, 2000), *Improving Your Credit and Reducing Your Debt* (Wiley, 1994), the *Short and Simple Guide to Life Insurance* (Authors Choice, 2000), and the *Short and Simple Guide to Smart Investing* (Authors Choice, 2003).

The two have contributed to *Consumers Digest, Your Money,* and *Worth* magazines, as well as the *Journal of the National Association of Personal Financial Advisors, Financial Advisor,* and *Financial Planning magazine.* Both are contributing editors for *Financial Advisor* magazine.

Liberman's own column, "Managing Your Fortune," runs in the *Palm Beach Daily News.* She helped found *Bank Rate Monitor* (now Bankrate.com) in North Palm Beach and was editor of the publication for 15 years. An award-winning journalist, she launched her career with the Associated Press, United Press International, and United Feature Syndicate. She also was a reporter for the *Courier-Post,* a Gannett newspaper in Cherry Hill, New Jersey. Liberman obtained her Bachelor's degree in journalism from Rutgers University, in New Brunswick, New Jersey. She holds a Florida real estate license and a Florida mortgage broker license.

Alan Lavine, author of the nation's longest-running mutual fund column, was on the ground floor of the mutual fund industry as the former director of research for IBC/Donoghue, now iMoneyNet.com, of Westborough, Massachusetts. His mutual fund column, in the *Boston Herald,* has been running for 20 years. He also pens a regular column for the *Journal of the National Association of Personal Financial Advisors* and has written for *The New York Times, Individual Investor, American Banker, American Lawyer,* and *Financial World.* During the 1980s, his family finances research was cited by the Joint Economic Committee of Congress. A frequent guest lecturer at Cornell University, Lavine has spoken before such groups as the American Psychology Association, the American Association for the Advancement of Science, the Massachusetts Psychological Association, and Morningstar, Inc.'s Mutual Fund Conference.

Lavine has a Master's degree from the University of Akron. He did post-graduate studies in finance and economics at Clark University, in Worcester, Massachusetts. Lavine has authored *Getting Started in Mutual Funds* (Wiley, 1993); *50 Ways to Mutual Fund Profits* (McGraw-Hill, 1996); *Your Life Insurance Options* (Wiley, 1992); *Diversify Your Way to Wealth* (McGraw-Hill, 1993), an alternate selection of the Fortune Book Club; and *Diversify: Investors Guide to Asset-Allocation Strategies* (Dearborn, 1989).

Both Liberman and Lavine are listed in Marquis's *Who's Who in America* and are members of the Society of American Business Editors and Writers.

Index

A

AARP (American Association of Retired Persons), 179
abroad settlements, 12-19
  car insurance, 19
  estate taxes, 19
  health care issues, 14-16
  paying taxes, 16-18
  property and joint ownership, 84
  real estate issues, 18-19
  retirement of William and Elizabeth Schrader, 1-19
  top 15 places to retire, 19
  accessory units, ECHO units, 121-122
ACCRA (American Chamber of Commerce Researchers Association), 150
age of retirement, 63
agency on aging, 48
AHCCCS (Arizona Health Care Cost Containment program), 57
allotments, land allotments (Native Americans), 166-167
American Association of Retired Persons. *See* AARP
American Century Short-Term Government Fund. *See* TWUSX
American Chamber of Commerce Researchers Association. *See* ACCRA
American Council of Life Insurance, 102
annual lease fees, living on a boat, 34
annuities
  fixed annuities, 83
  immediate annuities, 103
Arizona Health Care Cost Containment program. *See* AHCCCS

B

bank deposits, 81
  CDs (certificates of deposit), 81
  MMDAs (money market deposit accounts), 81
Barnard, Victor and Ruth, Co-housing retirement, 105-117
Belize, retirement of Edgar and Betty Plunkett, 69-80
  Belize Retirement Guide, 72
  Belize Retirement Program, 79
benefits, federal benefits of retirement, 62

alternative health-care solutions, 66-67
food stamp programs, 67
Medicaid, 64-66
Medicare, 64
Social Security, 63-64
SSI (Supplemental Security Income), 67
Blessings for a Long Time, 155
boat survey fee, living on a boat, 33
bond funds, 81
bribery, Mexico, 6
Bureau of Land Management, 99

C

Canadian Home Income Plan. *See* CHIP
car insurance, foreign countries, 19
car ownership costs, 46-47
cash value, life insurance policies, 173
Cashing in on the American Dream: How to Retire at 35, 183
catamarans, 35
CDs (certificates of deposit), 81
certificates of deposit. *See* CDs
CHIP (Canadian Home Income Plan), 179
Civil Service retirement system, 22
Clark, Alan and Sandra, early retirement and full-time travel, 87-98
Co-housing, 117-118

accessory units, ECHO units, 121-122
Cohousing Network, 117
commune-style housing, 118-119
match-up programs, 121
retirement of Victor and Ruth Barnard, 105-117
shared-living residence programs, 120-121
Commissioners 1980 Standard Ordinary Mortality Table, 102
commune-style housing, 118-119
community membership, Nyland Cohousing community, 110
Cooperative Housing Corporation, Matlin, Marjorie, 120
costs
car ownership, 46-47
living on a boat, 33-34
counseling, reverse mortgages, 180
credit unions, 81
Cruise Ship Crews, 50
cruise ship employment, 50
cruising sailboats, 35
Cruising World, 23, 34

D

Dawes Act of 1887, 165
Denman, Stanley E, qualifying for disability income, 168
determining retirement age, 63
dining out in Mexico, 9
disability, early retirement, 165

Index

maintaining a positive attitude, 168
qualifying for Social Security, 167-168
retirement of Dennis Hastings, 155-165
docking fees, living on a boat, 33
dream homes, Mark, Duane and Dolores, 53-62
Dreyfus Short-Intermediate Term Government Fund. *See* DSIGX
DSIGX (Dreyfus Short-Intermediate Term Government Fund), 82

E

early retirement assets, 152
  considering interest rates, 152
  determining lifestyle, 151
  disability, 165-168
    maintaining a positive attitude, 168
    qualifying for Social Security, 167-168
    retirement of Dennis Hastings, 155-165
  effects of inflation, 153
  Ferstenou, Larry and Kris, 143-151
  goals, 152
  immediate annuities, 103
  IRAs, 153
  listing monthly expenses, 152
  low-risk investments, 80-83
    bank deposits, 81
    bond funds, 81
    credit unions, 81
    fixed annuities, 83
    insured municipal bonds, 82-83
    money market mutual funds, 81
    short-term government bonds, 81-82
    treasury securities, 80
  making money last, 191-196
    decreasing expenses, 192-196
    index funds, 192
  Monforte, Alejandro and Letty, 123-134
  Plunkett, Edgar and Betty, 69-80
  quiz for early retirement, 196-197
  relocation, 151
  Social Security benefits, 101-103
  Terhorst, Paul and Vicki, 183-191
EBT cards (electronic benefits transfer cards), 67
ECHO (Elder Cottage Housing Opportunity) units, 122
Elder Cottage Housing Opportunity. *See* ECHO units
electronic benefits transfer cards. *See* EBT cards
employer sponsorship, obtaining a permanent visa, 135-136
estate taxes, foreign countries, 19
expenses
  consideration for early retirement, 152

reducing monthly expenses, 192-195

F

family member sponsorship, obtaining a permanent visa, 137-139
Fannie Mae (Federal National Mortgage Association), 179
federal benefits of retirement, 62-67
  alternative health-care solutions, 66-67
  food stamp programs, 67
  Medicaid, 64-66
  Medicare, 64
  Social Security, 63-64
  SSI (Supplemental Security Income), 67
Federal Housing Administration. *See* FHA Federal Housing Authority
loans, 50
Federal National Mortgage Association. *See* Fannie Mae
Fellowship for Intentional Community, 117
Ferstenou, Larry and Kris, early retirement, 143-151
FFLTX (Franklin Insured Tax-Free Income A), 83
FHA (Federal Housing Administration), reverse mortgages, 179
Financial Freedom Senior Funding Corporation, 179
"First Preference" (family preference sponsorship category), obtaining a permanent visa via family sponsorship, 137
fixed annuities, 83
FM2 immigration category, 5
FM3 immigration category, 4
food stamp programs, 67
"Fourth Preference" (family preference sponsorship category), obtaining a permanent visa via family sponsorship, 137
Frankl, Dr. Viktor Emil, 169
Franklin Insured Tax-FreeIncome A. *See* FFLTX
fuel costs, living on a boat, 33
full-time travel
  Clark, Alan and Sandra, 87-98
  RV travel, 98-101

G

General Allotment Act, 165
gift taxes, property and joint ownership, 84
Goldstein, Andrew J., maritime law, 32
government-subsidized low-rent apartments, 47
green cards
  obtaining a permanent visa, 134-139
    employer sponsorship, 135-136
    family member sponsorship, 137-139
    green card lottery, 134-135
  temporary visas, 136

Index

Grey, Bill and Claire, 72

H

H-1B temporary work visas, 136
H-2B temporary work visas, 136
Hastings, Dennis, early retirement due to disability, 155-165
health care coverage, 66-67
   foreign countries, 6-7, 14-16
   indemnity policies, 195
   Medicaid, 64-66
   Medicare, 64
   TRICARE for Life, 112
homeowner's fees, Mexico, 11
Hotwire website, 194
houseboats, 34
housing finance agency, 48
HUD (U.S. Department of Housing and Urban Development), 49

I

immediate annuities, 103
immigration
   finding a good employer, 139
   FM2 immigration category, 5
   FM3 immigration category, 4
   obtaining a permanent visa, 134-139
      employer sponsorship, 135-136
      family member sponsorship, 137-139
      green card lottery, 134-135
   retirement of Alejandro and Letty Monforte, 123-134

IMMS (Instituto Mexicano del Seguro Social), 12
income taxes, Mexico, 11
indemnity policies (health insurance), 195
index funds, 187, 192
Indian Land Tenure Foundation, 165
individual retirement accounts. *See* IRAs
inflation, consideration for early retirement, 153
information resources, reverse mortgages, 180
inspection fee, living on a boat, 33
Instituto Mexicano del Seguro Social. *See* IMMS
insurance boat, 33
   car, settling abroad, 19
   foreign countries, 6-7, 14-16
   health care coverage foreign countries, 6-7, 14-16
   indemnity policies, 195
   Medicaid, 64-66
   Medicare, 64
   TRICARE for Life, 112
insured municipal bonds, 82-83
intentional communities, 117-122
   accessory units, ECHO units, 121-122
   co-housing, 107
   commune-style housing, 118-119
   match-up programs, 121
   shared-living residence programs, 120-121

interest rates
  bankrate.com, 81
  consideration for early retirement, 152
investments, 191
  index funds, 187, 192
  low-risk, 80-83
    bank deposits, 81
    bond funds, 81
    credit unions, 81
    fixed annuities, 83
    insured municipal bonds, 82-83
    money market mutual funds, 81
    short-term government bonds, 81-82
    treasury securities, 80
IRAs (individual retirement accounts), 88, 153
issuers of reverse mortgages, FHA, 179

J

jointly owned property, 84

K

Kiss My Tears Away (Schrader), 2

L

Lake Chapala Society, 2
land allotments (Native Americans), 166-167
Landon, Mark, 50
Leach, James, 107
Liberman, Herman, retirement as a dance host, 37-46

life expectancy
  calculators, websites, 102
  tables, Commissioners 1980 Standard Ordinary Mortality Table, 102
Life Insurance Fact Book, 102
life insurance policies, cash value, 173
Life on Wheels school, Maxwell, Gaylord, 98
Liveaboard Magazine, 34
liveaboards, Murphy, Thomas, 21-32
Living Aboard, 34
living on a boat, 32-34
  cost of living, 33-34
  maintaining registration, 33
  maritime law, 32
  Murphy, Thomas, 21-32
living trusts, settling abroad, 19
loans, reverse mortgages, 178-180
  counseling, 180
  information resources, 180
  issuers, 179
low-cost places to live, 47-50
low-risk investments, 80-83
  bank deposits, 81
    CDs (certificates of deposit), 81
    MMDAs (money market deposit accounts), 81
  bond funds, 81
  credit unions, 81
  fixed annuities, 83
  insured municipal bonds, 82-83
  money market mutual funds, 81

182

Index

short-term government bonds, 81-82
treasury securities, 80
lump sum pension, 1

M

Maddox, Kathleen, reverse mortgage retirement, 171-178
magazines, retirement
　Cruising World, 34
　Liveaboard Magazines, 34
　Living Aboard, 34
　Modern Maturity, 19
Man's Search for Meaning, 169
marina docking fees, living on a boat, 33
maritime law, 32
Mark, Duane and Dolores, building of their dream home, 53-62
Marlin, Marjorie, Cooperative Housing Corporation, 120
match-up programs, 121
Maxwell, Gaylord, 98
Medicaid, 64-66
medical care, 66-67
　foreign countries, 6-7, 14-16
　indemnity policies, 195
　Medicaid, 64-66
　Medicare, 64
　TRICARE for Life, 112
Medicare, 64
Medigap policies, 64
Mexico
　bribery, 6
　retirement of William and Elizabeth Schrader, 1-19

MMDAs (money market deposit accounts), 81
Modern Maturity, top 15 places to retire abroad, 19
Money magazine, 20 best companies to work for in United States, 140
money market deposit accounts. *See* MMDAs
money market mutual funds, 81
Monforte, Alejandro and Letty, early retirement, 123-134
monthly annuity (pension), 1
monthly expenses, consideration for early retirement, 152
mortgages, reverse mortgages, 178-180
　counseling, 180
　information resources, 180
　issuers, 179
　retirement of Kathleen Maddox, 171-178
municipal bonds, insured municipal bonds, 82-83
Murphy, Thomas, retirement on a sailboat, 21-32
mutual funds, money market mutual funds, 81

N

National Council of State Housing Finance Agencies. *See NCSUA*
National Resource and Policy Center on Housing and Long Term Care, 120

National Reverse Mortgage Lenders Association, 180
National Shared Housing Resource Center, Zadoff, Rita, 121
Native Americans, land allotments, 166-167
NCSHA (National Council of State Housing Finance Agencies), 48
Nyland Cohousing community, retirement of Victor and Ruth Barnard, 105-117

O

Omaha Tribal Historical Research Project. *See* OTHRP
onboard retirement (retirement on a sailboat), 21-34
   cost of living, 33-34
   maintaining registration, 33
   maritime law, 32
   Murphy, Thomas, 21-32
1001 Ways to Cut Your Expenses, 193
OTHRP (Omaha Tribal Historical Research Project), 155

P

Part A (Medicare), 64
PartB (Medicare), 64
paying taxes, foreign countries, 16-18
pensions, receiving lump sum versus monthly annuity, 1

permanent visas, obtaining a permanent visa, 134-139
   employer sponsorship, 135-136
   family member sponsorship, 137-139
   green card lottery, 134-135
perpetual travelers, retirement of Paul and Vicki Terhorst, 183-191
Phillips, Lee R., 84
Pinney, Tor, 34
planning early retirement
   assets, 152
   considering interest rates, 152
   determining lifestyle, 151
   effects of inflation, 153
   Ferstenou, Larry and Kris, 143-151
   goals, 152
   IRAs, 153
   listing monthly expenses, 152
   Plunkett, Edgar and Betty, 69-80
   relocation, 151
Pond, Jonathan, 193
PPNs (preferred provider networks), 148
preferred provider networks. *See* PPNs
prescriptions, Mexico, 9
Priceline website, 194
Principal Financial Group, 10
   top-rated companies to work for, 139-140
property and joint ownership, 84
property taxes, Mexico, 11
Protecting Your Financial Future, 84
public housing authority, 48

Index

R

Ready for Sea! How to Outfit the Modern Cruising Sailboat, 34
real estate
    foreign countries, 18-19
    Mexico, 8
real estate investment trusts. *See* REITs
reducing monthly expenses, 192-196
registration, maintaining while living on a sailboat, 33
REITs (real estate investment trusts), 146
relocation, early retirement, 151
rent-controlled apartments, 49
rental housing, finding low-cost places to live, 47-50
resources, reverse mortgages, 180
Retire Early—and Live the Life You Want Now, 151
retirement age, 63
reverse mortgages, 178-180
    counseling, 180
    information resources, 180
    issuers, FHA, 179
    retirement of Kathleen Maddox, 171-178
RV travel, 98-101
    disadvantages, 100-101
    retirement of Alan and Sandra Clark, 87-98

S

Savings Incentive Match Plan for Employees. *See* SIMPLE plans
savings plans, Murphy, Thomas, 22
Schaub, Laird, Fellowship for Intentional Community, 117
Schrader, William and Elizabeth, retirement in Mexico, 1-19
"Second Preference" (family preference sponsorship category), obtaining a permanent visa via family sponsorship, 137
SEP accounts (simplified employee pension accounts), 88
settling abroad, 12-19
    car insurance, 19
    estate taxes, 19
    health care issues, 14-16
    Modern Maturity, 19
    paying taxes, 16-18
    property and joint ownership, 84
    real estate issues, 18-19
    retirement of William and Elizabeth Schrader, 1-19
    top 15 places to retire, 19
shared-living residence programs, 120-121
short-term government bonds, 81-82
SIMPLE plans (Savings Incentive Match Plan for Employees), 147
simplified employee pension accounts. *See* SEP accounts
Snyder, Vincent, 163
Social Security, 63-64
    benefits

disability checks, 167-168
taking Social Security early, 101-103
Social Security Administration, contact information, 102
special use permits, accessory units, 122
SSI (Supplemental Security Income), 67
Stainbrook, Chris, Indian Land Tenure Foundation, 165
state housing finance agency, 48
Supplemental Security Income. *See* SSI

T

taxes
estate taxes, settling abroad, 19
gift taxes, property and joint ownership, 84
paying taxes while living abroad, 16-18
temporary visas, 136
Terhorst, Paul and Vicki, perpetual travelers, 183-191
"Third Preference" (family preference sponsorship category), obtaining a permanent visa via family sponsorship, 137
thrift savings plan, Murphy, Thomas, 22
travel
finding lowest travel prices, websites, 194
full-time

Clark, Alan and Sandra, 87-98
RV travel, 98-101
Terhorst, Paul and Vicki, 183-191
world travelers
costs of car ownership, 46-47
cruise ship employment, 50
Liberman, Herman, 37-46
low-cost places to live, 47-50
TravelZoo website, 194
trawlers, 35
treasury securities, 80
TRICARE for Life, 112
trusts, settling abroad, 19
TWUSX (American Century Short-Term Government Fund), 82

U

U.S. Bureau of Land Management, 99
U.S. Coast Guard, 32
U.S. Department of Housing and Urban Development. *See* HUD
U.S. Department of Veteran Affairs, 67
U.S. Treasury securities, 80
utility charges, living on a boat, 34

V

Vanguard Insured Long-Term Tax-Exempt Fund. *See* VILPX
Vanguard Short-Term Federal. *See* VSGBX
Veteran Affairs, 67

Veteran's Administration loans, 50
VILPX (Vanguard Insured Long-Term Tax-Exempt Fund), 83
visas
    obtaining a permanent visa, 134-139
        employer sponsorship, 135-136
        family member sponsorship, 137-139
        green card lottery, 134-135
    temporary visa, 136
VSGBX (Vanguard Short-Term Federal), 82

W

Wasik John E, 151
WebFlyer website, 194
websites
    ACCRA (American Chamber of Commerce Researchers Association), 150
    bankrate.com, 81
    cohousing.com, 117
    Escapeartist.com, 185
    finding lowest travel prices, 194
    freecampgrounds.com, 99
    HUD (U.S. Department of Housing and Urban Development), 50
    life expectancy calculators
        healthcentral.com, 102
        moneycentral.msn.com, 102
    Living Aboard, 34
    National Reverse Mortgage Lenders Association, 180
    National Shared Housing Resource Center, 121
    NCSHA (National Council of State Housing Finance Agencies), 48
    publiclands.com, 99
    reverse mortgage counseling agencies, 180
    Social Security Administration, 102
    taxsites.com, 47
wills, settling abroad, 19
Wilson, J. Stephen, 135
Win the Green Card Lottery, 135
world travelers
    costs of car ownership, 46-47
    cruise ship employment, 50
    Liberman, Herman, 37-46
    low-cost places to live, 47-50

X

xeriscapes, 112

Y

Yale-Loehr, Stephen, immigration law, 134
You Can Retire Young, 144

Z

Zadoff, Rita, National Shared Housing Resource Center, 121

Manufactured By: RR Donnelley
Momence, IL USA
January, 2011